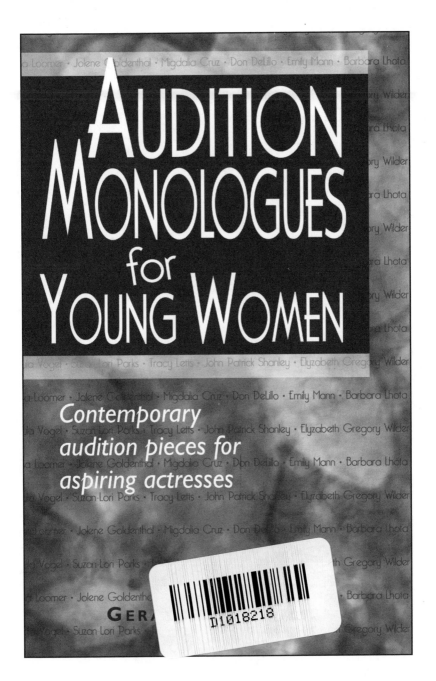

AUDITION MONOLOGUES
for YOUNG WOMEN

Contemporary
audition pieces for
aspiring actresses

GER...

D1018218

MERIWETHER PUBLISHING LTD.
Colorado Springs, Colorado

Meriwether Publishing Ltd., Publisher
PO Box 7710
Colorado Springs, CO 80933-7710

www.meriwether.com

Executive editor: Theodore O. Zapel
Assistant editor: Amy Hammelev
Cover design: Jan Melvin

© Copyright MMXI Meriwether Publishing Ltd.
Printed in the United States of America
First Edition

All rights reserved. No part of this publication may be reproduced, stored in a retrieval system, or transmitted in any form or by any means, electronic, mechanical, photocopying, recording or otherwise, without permission of the publishers.

CAUTION: Professionals and amateurs are hereby warned that the plays and monologues represented in this book are subject to royalty. They are fully protected under the copyright laws of the United States of America and of all countries covered by the International Copyright Union (including the Dominion of Canada and the rest of the British Commonwealth), and of all countries covered by the Pan-American Copyright Convention, the Universal Copyright Convention, the Berne Convention and of all other countries with which the United States has reciprocal copyright relations. All rights, including professional/amateur stage rights, motion picture, recitation, lecturing, public reading, radio broadcasting, television, video or sound recording, all other forms of mechanical or electronic reproduction, such as CD-ROM, CD-I, information storage and retrieval systems and photocopying, and the rights of translation into foreign languages, are strictly reserved. Particular emphasis is laid upon the question of readings, permission for which must be secured from the author's agent in writing. These plays and monologues may not be publicly performed without express written permission from the author or the author's agent. Pages 165-172 constitute an extension of this copyright page.

Library of Congress Cataloging-in-Publication Data

Ratliff, Gerald Lee.
    Audition monologues for young women : contemporary audition pieces for aspiring actresses / by Gerald Lee Ratliff. -- 1st ed.
        p. cm.
    ISBN 978-1-56608-180-1
    1. Monologues. 2. Acting--Auditions. 3. Women--Drama. I. Title.
    PN2080.R368 2011
    812'.045089287--dc23

                                    2011029308

1   2   3   11   12   13

CONTENTS

PRELUDE

*"Imagination, Industry, and Intelligence — the Three I's —
are all indispensable to the actor, but of these three the greatest is,
without any doubt, Imagination."*
— Ellen Terry, *Memoirs*

This new collection of monologues and duo scenes features a number of familiar theatre voices and a host of new voices that are just now beginning to emerge. All of the playwrights, however, share a common denominator: They offer fresh, imaginative character portraits for young women that capture vivid attitudes, images, and speeches of realistic characters drawn from real-life role models.

A number of the excerpts are original, independent, unpublished monologues or duo scenes featuring recognizable visual portraits of authentic people, places, and events. These honest, truthful depictions of contemporary life focus attention on the social forces that help to shape a character's behavior or direct attention to actions and attitudes that reveal a character's point of view.

The excerpts are grouped in chapters framed by themes, rather than by age range or genre. A brief background sketch provides an initial glimpse of the given circumstances, emotional or intellectual tenor, and performance hints for each monologue or duo scene. Although independent of the original text, monologues and duo scenes capture the emotional and intellectual complexities of each excerpt and offer striking images that help to shape each character portrait.

There is a range of literary styles and thematic storylines in this collection to challenge you in acting assignments, classroom discussions, or formal auditions. There are character sketches that depict realistic tales of greed, betrayal, self-sacrifice, and genuine faith, as well as absurdist comedies, social dramas, satiric riffs on dysfunctional relationships, and timely comments on the ills of society. There is also an assortment of vivid human experiences — violence, intrigue, revenge, romance, rejection, and the indomitable spirit of survival expressed in personal, philosophical, or poetic terms by the gifted playwrights who appear to inhabit the real world, which they evoke in their characters.

Now you, the actor, must breathe life and meaning into these monologues and duo scenes, give voice to the characters, and communicate a deeper understanding of the inimitable wit, resilient strength, or sense of fear and hope in these imaginary lives. Probe deeply into the secret thoughts of characters that speak to your heart as well as to your mind. Identify the sense of humor, misguided hopes, frustrated dreams, or sad truths that are tattooed on each self-portrait. Focus on what the characters are trying to accomplish in the script and play the *action* of the given circumstances with a degree of comprehensive understanding and a measure of artistic control in order to achieve each character's primary *objective* in the monologue or duo scene.

— Gerald Lee Ratliff

CHAPTER I
AUDITION ETIQUETTE

"When student-actors see people and the way they behave when together, see the color of the sky, hear the sounds in the air, feel the ground beneath them and the wind on their faces, they get a wider view of their personal world and development in the theatre is quickened. The world provides the material for the theatre and artistic growth develops hand-in-hand with one's recognition of it and one's self within it."
— Viola Spolin, *Improvisation for the Theatre*

Preparing for a theatre audition involves more than quickly selecting a random monologue and memorizing the character's dialogue. It is just as important to be aware of audition etiquette and be prepared for any unanticipated requests made by the director. Your choice of monologues should exhibit an emotional or intellectual range that is compatible with your life experiences.

Select characters whose emotional depth or intellectual curiosity you can clearly define and understand. Honest and simple — rather than slick and polished — are basic ingredients for all auditions. Approach the audition in a calm, relaxed manner. Strive to live moment-to-moment in your character's brief audition life. Explore monologue characters that exhibit variety in their emotions and must overcome significant obstacles in their internal or external struggle.

Always read monologues *aloud* before making character choices. Do you *hear* the character's conflict, or is it just heated conversation? Do you *see* the character's physical struggle, or is it simply resignation to what has already happened? Do you *feel* the character's emotional anguish, or is your response essentially a sympathetic identification with the circumstances? Do you *sense* the character's climactic build to a resolution of conflict, or is there merely a slight change in attitude or mood?

First Steps

One of the first steps in previewing potential audition monologues is to read and analyze the script. If you hope to create a believable character portrait, it is crucial to know and understand a character's changing attitude or mood in the complete storyline rather than in just an isolated monologue or duo scene. Unless you become familiar with the series of complex incidents that motivate a character's action, your audition interpretation and performance may fall flat because it lacks sustained believability, continuity, and depth of understanding.

Reading the complete text of a play as a prelude to understanding the character's intent or motivation is one of the root ideas of script analysis and interpretation. When you read the complete text, pay special attention to what the character "says" or "does" and a fictional life history should surface. This background information may later inform why a character behaves or speaks in a certain manner within the context of a given situation or in making a specific decision.

Another step that may be helpful is to initially define a character's intention or motivation with active *verbs* that give vocal color and meaning to the dialogue. Identifying the changing pattern of a character's attitude, mood, or word choice in the complete script may also help you visualize the conflict described in a potential monologue or duo scene. Examples of some active verbs to describe a character's intention or motivation might include: to seduce, to ridicule, to expose, to humiliate, to confuse, to conquer, to overcome, or simply to survive.

Trying to visualize a potential audition monologue while reading the complete text is like reading the notes of a printed score of music: find the rhythm. Each monologue should have its own "beat" and "tempo," or speed, based solely upon the character's words and actions. Read a script as you might read a novel or short story by sorting out the characters and the storyline. Chart the build to a climax and focus on character relationships caught up in the action. Pay particular attention to vivid images and subtle changes in attitude or mood that might highlight or give an additional meaning to a character's intention and motivation.

There are a number of final steps to consider when you review potential audition monologues. First, look for monologues that have one climactic moment, a series of striking turning points, and obvious conflict (internal or external). Second, look for monologues that encourage you to make performance choices that build moment-to-moment anticipation and suspense.

Third, look for monologues that actively engage your voice and body in mental *and* physical activity in order to play character "actions" rather than "emotions." Fourth, look for monologues that have a rising rhythm or tempo that underscores a character's attitude or mood and also presents meaningful opportunities for movement. Fifth, look for monologues with a storyline that has time to build momentum and engage audience attention.

As you gain more experience in reading the complete text of a script, your ability to respond to potential monologue character clues will increase. There are, however, a number of pitfalls to avoid in your preview. As a general rule of thumb, avoid monologues filled with excessive past tense narration. "Telling a story" without any specific character *actions* to indicate the build to a climax is essentially an exercise in reading aloud or oral interpretation of literature.

Identify only those monologue characters that represent your age range — usually within six to eight years of your own age — and physical type. Select monologues that engage you on an emotional or intellectual level, but avoid those monologues that use crude or sexually explicit language. Dismiss "Once upon a time" and "I remember when" monologues that relive past events or recall past experiences and feature the actor as a storyteller rather than as an active participant engaged in the immediate unfolding of the character's action or conflict.

At the same time, exclude monologues that rely on elaborate costumes, hand props, or sound effects to visualize a character portrait. Learn to avoid monologues that call for special accents or dialects as well. It is also a good idea to avoid funny voices or goofy walks to suggest a comic character. True humor usually surfaces when the character is deep in the given circumstances of a text and is reaching a level of pain or even panic that leads to those circumstances spinning wildly — comically — out of control.

Finally, make sure that your audition monologue can stand alone as an individual episode or incident that has a beginning, middle, and end. In other words, a monologue is a character's journey of self-discovery, unfolding moment to moment, that actively engages the actor as a participant in a series of meaningful *experiences,* not just observations. Monologue characters who spend precious time on-stage recalling past events to define themselves are engaged in "narrative exposition," so avoid those types whose passion is to talk rather than to take action, overcome an obstacle, or resolve a conflict.

Basic Principles

There is more involved in the audition process than exhibiting some spontaneous creativity. The following basic principles are essential ingredients to consider when you have identified a number of monologues that might be appropriate for an audition. One of the first principles is to make performance choices that clearly define each of your monologue characters. Individual choices should identify the (a) incident being described, (b) apparent conflict, (c) language and word choices, (d) emotional moments, and (e) mental state of the character and given circumstances.

Another principle to cultivate is a positive audition attitude through careful preparation and rehearsal. A positive audition attitude suggests a risk-taking, spirited, and inventive actor with a hint of uninhibited abandon. Of course, we are all more critical of ourselves if we lack initial confidence in our ability to "perform" before an audience, especially when that audience appears as a sea of strange faces. But the truth — which you will soon discover as your own self-confidence and poise matures — is that *all* performers begin as awkward, timid novices.

Please review the following ingredients that are standard practices when you audition for a director. Remember, however, that there are as many approaches to conducting an audition as there are theatre directors. Some directors use a *cold reading,* where the actor is given a prepared character speech and asked to perform the excerpt with little or no time for preparation. A cold reading gives the director an initial impression of your basic skills in dialogue interpretation and vocal or physical range.

Other directors prefer the *prepared reading,* where an actor performs two brief, contrasting monologues from different historical periods (Classical Greek, Roman, Shakespeare, or Contemporary, for example). The prepared reading helps a director identify a pool of potential talent available for possible callbacks and focuses attention on each actor's ability to clearly delineate character attitudes or moods. Still other directors prefer auditions that are *open* to all interested actors or *closed* and only those who have been invited may participate.

A *general* audition, however, is the most common type and is used to "screen" a number of actors for a more intensive review at a later callback. Each type of audition may also include improvisational activities, a sequence of impromptu exercises or theatre games, or a *directed reading,* where the director gives specific instructions in interpretation or movement before asking actors to perform a solo character speech or a duo scene from the script being cast.

Here are some basic assumptions to consider as part of your pre-audition rehearsal. These traditional approaches should guide you in preparing an audition that meets standard expectations but also gives vitality to your performance. Too many actors make an initial error in judgment when they fail to consider traditional audition practices *before* selecting their monologues. Please review the following features of audition etiquette and make appropriate adjustments in your audition preparation during the rehearsal period.

Introduction

The first "performance moment" of an audition is to introduce yourself and the monologue(s) you are performing. The spoken introduction is memorized and should be brief — thirty seconds is sufficient — but marked with a personal signature of self-confidence. A sample introduction might simply be, "Hello. My name is ____. I'll be doing a monologue from Tennessee Williams' *The Glass Menagerie.*" You may also choose to indicate the name of the monologue character and the setting if time permits.

Time

Think of the audition as a professional appointment and always be punctual. Anticipate arriving early for your appointment — and never arrive late. Review the monologue text or warm up with vocal and physical relaxation exercises while waiting to have your name called. Time also refers to the minutes allocated for each monologue audition — usually two to three minutes — so respect the time limit and make cuts in the text as required.

7

Wardrobe

An appropriate audition wardrobe subtly reflects the attitude or mood of the monologue character. The wardrobe should be carefully selected in terms of cut, style, and color to enhance your physical dimensions. Warm and soft colors are particularly effective. Avoid the tendency to wear theatrical costumes to an audition and focus on traditional designer principles of line, texture, and simple ornament. Remember that a carefully selected wardrobe can suggest a monologue character's lifestyle or sense of self.

Props

Hand props should be clearly indicated in the text and limited to specific — and small — objects that are easily handled and a logical extension of the monologue character. Do not litter the stage with an assortment of hand props that may later become part of your audition. An audition is never about props or other theatrical accessories. An audition is about you and how to fill an empty space using only yourself as a prop.

Makeup

Light street makeup or a warm bronzer is always appropriate for women to wear at auditions. Hair, however, should be kept away from the face so expressions are clearly seen. Do not rely on elaborate accessories such as wigs or hair extensions, and avoid wearing platform shoes, flip-flops, or high heels that tend to make movement appear awkward and unnatural. The role of makeup in an audition is to accent facial expressions with a hint of color.

Accents

Auditions are almost always performed in standard American speech that is free of colloquialism, regionalism, or distracting speech patterns. Use character accents only if they can be voiced with authenticity and accuracy. To cultivate a working catalogue of familiar audition accents (British, Cockney, Italian, or Southern American, for example), it may be useful to purchase accent tapes, learn the phonetic alphabet, or view film clips that feature ethnic accents.

Focus

It is not a good idea to use specific individuals or vacant seats in the audience to represent the characters you may be addressing in the monologue. The role of *off-stage focus,* however, may be very useful in an audition setting. Off-stage focus places the location of characters or incidents on a straight or angled line slightly above the heads of the audience. Off-stage focus also places the actor in a prominent, full-front position and directs facial expressions and vocal responses forward toward the listeners.

Business

The role of active stage business to advance the storyline of a monologue is limited in an audition but, used effectively, can clearly establish a sense of character definition. Initial hints of stage business should be revealed in the text and not arbitrarily inserted into the monologue. Some familiar uses of stage business include handling small props like eyeglasses or cigarette cases, adjusting clothing, or exhibiting character behavioral habits and mannerisms like blinking, cracking knuckles, clearing one's throat, or scratching the head.

Staging

In staging an audition monologue you should anticipate a limited number of set pieces — perhaps a single chair, stool, and small table. Do not assume you can request additional set pieces, and do not consider monologues that require mood lighting, special effects, or a sound track. Movement in the playing space should be limited to focus attention on the monologue character's action. Set up the space so that you are facing the audience, and be careful not to deliver your entire monologue in profile.

Movement

Although stage movement may play a significant role in fleshing out a character portrait in full-length scripts, it is unlikely to have an immediate impact in an audition. You should, however, explore subtle movement opportunities in gesture, posture, or stance. A good audition blueprint maintains a careful balance between movement that helps to punctuate character action or underline character attitude and movement that accentuates the tempo or rhythm of both the text *and* the audition performance.

Pantomime

It takes a measure of discipline and professional training for a mime artist to perform, but an actor should never pantomime opening or closing an imaginary door, drinking from an invisible glass, puffing on a make-believe cigarette, or eating food from an empty table in an audition. No matter how well executed, pantomime is inadequate and unnecessary to convey the simple truth and honesty of a monologue character and does not accentuate what a character "says" or "does" in an audition performance.

Entrance

As soon as you enter the playing area, seize the space! Walk with an air of self-confidence and make direct eye contact with the audience. Go directly to center stage to introduce yourself and your monologue(s). If you need to move a chair or rearrange the playing space, do so quickly and quietly. It is perfectly acceptable for you to ask if the evaluator(s) would prefer that you perform the monologue directly to them or if they would simply rather observe.

Exit

Pause at the end of your audition, briefly hold the climactic moment of the monologue, and then simply say, "Thank you" and exit with the same poise that marked your self-confident entrance. Do not offer a dramatic bow and blurt out "Scene" or "That's it." Do not comment on your performance — especially to offer apologies, make excuses, or ask for feedback. There is no time or need for comments after an audition.

Additional Dimensions

Here are some additional dimensions to review as part of your pre-audition preparation. If you are performing two contrasting monologues, introduce both of them at the beginning and then use brief spoken transitions to move easily from one to the other. Transitions should also be memorized and include brief remarks that identify the character, setting, and situation. A typical transition for a second monologue in an audition might say, for example, "Isabel, a disillusioned young woman in Athol Fugard's *My Children! My Africa!*, shares her thoughts about a recent incident of racial violence with a former high school friend."

Although the primary source of material for monologues or short scenes is found in anthologies edited specifically for auditions, you should make use of the *acting edition* of a text if it is available. The acting edition is a documented history of the text and may include stage directions, performance notes, or occasional character interpretation clues that helped frame the text as it was revised in rehearsal or production. When you read the acting edition of a script, look for a monologue that captures a character at the height of conflict or wrestling with a difficult decision or painful situation — and that is the place to start the audition text. Acting editions of a script are relatively inexpensive and may be purchased directly from current catalogues of publishers like Dramatists Play Service, Inc., Samuel French, Inc., Theatre Communications Group, or Playscripts, Inc. (Please review the suggested list of Supplemental Resource Materials at the end of the book on page 161 for additional contact information on these and other valuable theatre resources.)

Rehearsing in the audition space before your scheduled call should also help you to experience a more comfortable and relaxed atmosphere in which to later perform. Explore the vocal and physical demands of the playing area, paying special attention to acoustics, exits and entrances, stage dimensions, and audience seating arrangement. If you are unable to gain prior access to a traditional theatre stage, rehearse in a number of different playing spaces — classroom, dance studio, gymnasium floor, recital hall, cafeteria — to anticipate auditions that may be held in a nontraditional space.

Preparing for a monologue audition also includes a rigorous rehearsal period to explore character interpretation and visualize character action suggested in the text. Some actors use the rehearsal period as a time to search for a *metaphor* — an implied comparison between the character and something inventive — that might give added dimension and meaning to the character portrait. Other actors use the rehearsal period to engage in *word play* with lines of dialogue to highlight and punctuate phrases or individual words spoken by the monologue character. A few actors use rehearsal time to visualize "action" words or images suggested in the text and then translate those words or images into a character's physical movement.

It may be helpful to think of the rehearsal period as a creative laboratory in which you experiment with different performance techniques in a search to discover new audition insights. The rehearsal period is also a good time to fill in any blanks left unanswered in the monologue or duo scene, especially if there are unresolved questions about a character's intention or motivation. Regardless of the approach you may choose to take in the rehearsal period, it is crucial to include regular sessions in vocal and physical exercise.

A rehearsal routine that regularly fine-tunes the voice and body helps combat the initial anxiety associated with an audition. Regular exercise is essential to condition the voice and body to respond effectively to any vocal or physical demand. A regular exercise schedule should help you cultivate more expressive vocal qualities and movement styles that give energy and vitality to your monologue character portraits.

There has been a significant movement recently toward nontraditional casting and a number of directors now look for actors to play roles that, in past practice, may not have been considered appropriate. Nontraditional casting is color-blind, with no preference given to race, gender, or ethnicity. (A number of monologues in this book are nontraditional and open to casting against type as well.) Nontraditional casting also presents performance opportunities for actors whose age, height, or physique are opposite of what a character role may appear to be at first glance.

Before selecting a final audition monologue, use a wristwatch with a second hand to time the text. Don't forget to allow time for an introduction, pauses, some brief transitions, and the build to a climax. You should also try to paraphrase the dialogue into conversational words and reduce the character's actions, thoughts, and ideas to one-word nouns or verbs that can be explored vocally *and* physically in rehearsal. It may also be useful to invent a brief imaginary biography that gives added dimension to your monologue character portrait.

Remember that the first twenty-five seconds of an audition are the most crucial in terms of indicating your potential range of emotional, physical, and vocal qualities. At the same time, the last twenty-five seconds may be just as crucial to reinforce a three-dimensional character portrait through subtle shifts in phrasing dialogue, vocal tone, and stage movement or gesture. That is why it is important to design an audition blueprint that mirrors the *stage world* of your monologue character, rather than simply "acting" or "reading aloud" on a bare stage or in an empty room.

Finally, don't be anxious about "going up"— forgetting your lines — during an audition. If you do forget your lines, be prepared through the rigor of the rehearsal period to paraphrase or improvise a monologue character's dialogue. You are the only person with a complete copy of the audition monologue, so learn to go on as if any momentary lapse is an integral part of your performance. Of course, you can reduce the possibility of forgetting lines if you focus on good memorization skills and practice dialogue aloud rather than silently.

Sample Monologues

The following sample monologues are original texts, not excerpts of character speeches from traditional full-length published playscripts. They are independent character sketches written to challenge you in classroom discussion and performance. The sample monologues share many of the same three-dimensional character life experiences and points of view that you would expect to find in a more complete script. Each sample presents distinctive character portraits that should stimulate your creative talents in a classroom setting.

Begin with a close reading of each monologue and identify those that best suit your age range, vocal quality, and physical type. Your first impressions should provide an initial glimpse of each character's "self-image," especially in terms of how you begin to visualize the character's action, attitude, or intention in the text. Using the character clues suggested in a brief introduction to each monologue, make some preliminary choices of character objectives that you will pursue in the rehearsal period.

When you have made these initial choices — informed by several readings of your favorite monologues — and practiced each speech in a rehearsal period, select *one* of the texts that you would like to explore as an audition monologue. Now give some thought to what role, if any, hand props, movement, or wardrobe might play in sketching a well-defined character portrait. Then experiment with different approaches to staging or character placement in the playing space, knowing that there may only be a chair, stool, or small table available to you in an audition. Finally, work on a brief, memorized introduction for the audition monologue.

At this point, you should have a good sense of basic monologue audition principles and standard etiquette practices. The experience and self-confidence you gain in translating these basic principles and practices into a more refined audition blueprint will be invaluable in polishing your interpretation and performance skills. Remember, however, that *honesty* and *simplicity* are the essential ingredients of success in an audition. Your ability to embrace these qualities should inspire an authentic and highly personal audition performance.

Role Playing

In playing these original monologue roles, pay particular attention to performance choices that highlight the "inner" and the "outer" character in terms of vocal and physical attributes. Encourage a natural and conversational tone of expression to give depth and dimension to character ideas, emotions, or thoughts. Display sensitivity to the action and situation described in the monologue and you will also help to clarify the subtext of the dialogue while underlining the character's attitude or mood.

Monologues with comic overtones also need to be approached with sensitivity so a heightened spirit of humor does not reduce characters to farcical, one-dimensional cardboard stereotypes. This should be done subtly and with a sense of restraint so there is still a comic spirit in the interpretation, but the humor does not detract from the character's point of view in attitude or action. It is much more important to isolate the "cause" of the comic spirit in order to understand the role humor plays in a monologue or duo scene and then use that humor to punctuate the *actions* of the character in a given situation.

Finally, some attention should be paid to the role that character facial expressions and physical reactions or responses play in an audition. Do not rely too heavily upon transparent facial expressions, physical reactions, or even vocal responses to convey a character's attitude or point of view. The visual portrait of a character needs to be clearly but subtly defined to indicate what the character may be thinking or even anticipating at any given moment. There are a number of performance clues in the introduction to each monologue and duo scene that should assist you in creating a dramatic sense of "telescoping" each character's intention or motivation in terms of attitude, mood, or point of view.

I Ate the Divorce Papers
by Gabriel Benjamin Davis

In this whimsical jewel, an unsuspecting wife, in the face of impending grief, holds a cracked mirror up to her marriage when served with divorce papers by her estranged husband. It is a surprisingly touching self-portrait filled with moments that all will recognize and lessons we all need to learn. It is also a memorable illustration of how we see ourselves ... and how others happen to see us. Obviously the husband and wife in this episode cast similar lights and shadows around themselves even though they appear to live in separate worlds.

JILLIAN: *(Standing in front of her soon to be ex-husband)* I ate them. That's right. I ate the divorce papers, Charles. I ate them with ketchup. And they were good ... gooood. You probably want me to get serious about our divorce. The thing is you always called our marriage a joke. So let's use logic here: If (A) we never had a serious marriage then (B) we can't have a serious divorce. No. We can't. The whole thing's a farce, Charles — a farce that tastes good with ketchup. *(Beat)*

I mean, wasn't it last week, your dad asked you the reason you walked down that aisle with me and you said, "for the exercise." Ha, ha. That's funny. You're a funny guy, Charles. I'm laughing, not crying. Ha, ha. I'm laughing because you're about to give up on a woman who is infinitely lovable. *(Beat)*

For instance: Paul. He has loved me since the eighth grade. Sure, he's a little creepy, but he reeeeally loves me. He's made one hundred twenty-seven passes at me, proposed forty-seven times, and sent me over two hundred original love sonnets. He sees something in me, Charles. And he writes it down, in metered verse! *(Beat)*

And that's not something you just find every day. Someone who really loves everything about who you are as a person. Paul may be insane, but I value his feelings for me. *(Beat)*

I would never ask him to sign his name to a piece of paper promising to just turn off his feelings for me forever. But that's what you are asking me to do, for you. To sign away my right to … to that sweet voice, Charles, those baby brown eyes, the way your hands feel through my hair before bed … *(Beat)*

Those aren't things I want to lose. In fact, I won't lose them. I won't lose you. I'll woo you. I've written you a sonnet. "Shall I compare thee to a summer's day. Thou art more lovely and more temperate, rough winds do shake the darling buds of May and … " I'm not crying. I'm laughing. It's all a big joke. It's very funny, Charles. I keep waiting for you to say, "April Fools." Then I'll rush into your arms and … But you're not going to, are you? No. Of course not. It's not April. *(Beat)*

I, I didn't really write that sonnet, you know. Paul did. I think it's good. *(Beat)* You see, the truth … The truth is, Charles, I ate the divorce papers … I ate them … because I can't stomach the thought of losing you.

Schoolhouse Rock
by Jason D. Martin

This remarkable elementary school teacher with all the answers is bubbly, bristling, and slightly eccentric as she passionately delivers her introductory lecture titled "Three things every little boy and girl should know" to a rapt audience of first grade students. In a series of short and thoroughly engaging pleas, Emily creates her own magical world to subvert any cherished hopes of a future the children may have anticipated. Her annual rant may "rock the schoolhouse" and produce explosions of derisive laughter from adults, but also raises serious questions about the need for an immediate and thorough examination of our educational system!

(Note: The actress playing the role should attempt to get the audience to repeat the given lines as if they are the young children in the first grade class.)

TEACHER: All right, children, everyone sit down. Mikey stop pulling Sarah's hair. Christopher … No. Please do not wipe snot on Julie. Settle down children. Today I want to tell you about three things every little boy and girl should know. These are very important things, so I want you all to sit with legs crossed and pay very close attention. Okay, first … Never ride with a stranger. This is very important so I want you all to repeat this rule to me. Never ride with a stranger. All together now. Ready?

Never ride with a stranger. Good. Why shouldn't we ride with a stranger? Julie? Very good, he might not be such a nice guy. He might be dangerous. You never know, a stranger might offer you candy … But then take you and put you in a box full of snakes … You just never know. Now let's say it one more time just to make sure that you all have it down. All together now: Never ride with a stranger. Good. Very good. Now the second thing: Always wear your seat belt. This is very important so I want you all to say it together with me. Always wear your seat belt. Ready? Together now: Always wear your seat belt. Now why do we always want to wear our seat belt? Mikey? Right … If you are in a car accident you could get hurt. Exactly. You might go through the windshield and get run over by an ice cream truck. You just never know. Now one more time, all together. Always wear your seat belt. Very good.

Now this is the last and most important thing to remember. You must listen very closely because it affects every one of you. You must also listen closely because I'm going to have you repeat it. Okay, kids, are you ready? Here goes: The governments of the world are involved in a multinational conspiracy with an alien race from the planet Zeon; the ultimate goal of this alliance being the total domination and conversion of every man, woman, and child on this planet into hosts for a future alien race that will use all mankind like cattle for food. Now are there any questions? Sarah? What is a multinational conspiracy? Well, that's when all the governments of the world get together to keep secrets from the people. The aliens are already among us … The government doesn't want you to know that you are all going to be fodder for an alien race. Remember how Miss Graham, your principal, told you that little Johnny White had to move away? Miss Graham is part of the conspiracy. What really happened is that the aliens took over

Johnny's mommy and daddy; and they in turn changed into alien monsters with huge teeth and giant claws.

When little Johnny went to bed, they were hiding. The mommy monster alien was under the bed and the daddy monster was in the closet. Little Johnny didn't even know what hit him. The monsters came out and started to tear that little boy to shreds. He screamed and screamed ... After they were done, they made a milkshake with his brain. Now are there any more questions? Oh, don't cry. Mikey? You're going to tell on me? To whom? Miss Graham? She's part of the conspiracy. She's an alien dressed up to look like a principal. Go ahead and tell her ... I wouldn't want to be in a room alone with her. She might suck your brain right out your ear. Any other questions? Christopher? I'm scaring you and you're going to tell your mommy and daddy? Well, Christopher ... What if your mommy and daddy have already been taken over by alien hosts? What it you go to them and say, "Mommy, Daddy, my teacher says that there are aliens among us!" And then what if they tie you down to the table and start to do experiments on you? You wouldn't want that would you?

Okay, now all together. The governments of the world are involved in a multinational conspiracy with an alien race from the planet Zeon; the ultimate goal of this alliance being the total domination and conversion of every man, woman, and child into hosts for a future alien race that will use all mankind like cattle for food. Very good. That was excellent for first graders! Now tomorrow we are going to talk about the letter "A," how to wash your hands correctly, and how to make a tinfoil hat that will keep the alien species from reading your mind. Have a good afternoon children and don't forget what we talked about today!

Rhyming *and* Driving
by David Moberg

These original monologues feature two unnamed, defiant women who offer a sly, at times whimsical, portrait of love that has surprising nuance and sudden surges of emotion — but just as quickly turns to a fiery brand of social satire. Despite the subject matter, these are funny vignettes that send an intriguing message to couples that are drifting apart and looking for a path that will lead them back to the light of day. Let's take a fresh look at two "star-crossed" lovers who come to terms with their rage in different ways and the men who are romantically involved in their lives.

WOMAN 1: *(Rhyming)* And then he died and I never cried. He would have liked that ... I rhymed. "You and I," he used to say, "we fit together like poetry. We rhyme; our meter matches; we're the perfect couplet." And then he'd hit me. Not hard at first; then he'd laugh; a kind of teasing laugh. And I'd laugh too so maybe he'd stop hitting me. "When you're with the best, you get no rest." And then he'd pin me down with his feet, standing over me. "You'll remember what I said if I write it in red." And he'd slap me all over until red welts, sometimes blood would ... I'd scream, "I love you. Why are you doing this?" "Talking back is like an attack!" And he threw something metal and I was in the hospital after that. "Girls who squeal gonna get a really raw deal." He was still rhyming.

I lied and told everyone that I fell down the stairs. That's why my scalp was split and six ribs cracked. So I left. Tried to anyway. "A rhyme once made must be true and staid." And he went to get his bat from the basement, all the time yelling ... "One hand; one heart; till death do us part." So I locked the car doors and started to back out of the garage. And he jumped right behind the tail pipe of my white Taurus and started bashing the trunk with the bat and screaming, "I told you to stay; I'm blocking your wicked way." And he shattered the back window. So I screamed, "Get off the track, Jack, I'm coming back."

Now he's crazy. "You gotta taste this wood so's you can listen real good." I punched the pedal and back I go ... fast, before he can get that bat at my face. And I hear this double thump, da dum, like an iambic stress, and his rhyming stopped. But I didn't. I kept the pedal down, hit the road, found a new town, and plan to grow old ... without ever reading a rhyming verse again.

WOMAN 2: *(Driving)* So I'm driving and he goes ... *(She demonstrates)* ... a little finger flick to the west which means ... go *his* way. See, I'm supposed to read his fingers so I can do what he wants without his having to waste breath actually talking to me ... But I'm driving, we're going *my* way. And now he's doing the wrist snap ... *(She demonstrates)* ... index finger extended, but I keep straight ahead, staring down that white road line. Next he's using the whole arm ... *(She demonstrates)* ... chopping from the elbow, with his bird fingernail flying against the inside of the glass pointing me to go *his* way. But I'm up to *here* ... If he wants me to turn, he needs to talk to me with his mouth!

And then he starts grabbing at his chest and his hands are up here like he's trying to scoop air down his throat ... And before I can even stop the car, he's barely twitching and his face is kinda fuzzy blue. So I drag him out of his seat belt, throw him across my lap and I'm pounding at his chest ... *(She demonstrates)* ... like I could beat the blood through his heart from the outside. Don't die, please don't die. But then I notice ... His fingers aren't pointing me what to do or where to go or whatever. So I stop. I prop him back up against the door, re-buckle his seat belt, and drive *my* way to the hospital — the long way. Very slowly ...

Dating Hamlet
by Bruce Kane

In this imaginative adaptation of Shakespeare's immortal tragedy Hamlet, *the focus is on the high-spirited and outlandishly humorous Ophelia, who offers a wry, witty examination of true love's ability to blossom under the most unlikely of circumstances. Determined to be a real live princess, or die, Ophelia is a youthful mixture of sophistication and romantic novice with a cool breeziness that covers, but never obscures, her inventive retelling of the romantic misadventures that she has clung to so desperately in the unending pursuit of Hamlet, Prince of Denmark.*

OPHELIA: "To be or not to be that is the question ... " *(Dropping the Shakespearean tone and replacing it with a modern sound.)* No, it's not ... That's not the question. That never was the question. The question is, "Will you marry me?" That's the question. But when you're with a guy who can't make up his mind about anything, what you get is "Whether 'tis nobler to suffer the slings and arrows of outrageous ..." Blah, blah, blah. What is with you guys anyway? Don't you know a good thing when it's right there in front of you? You always think something better is just around the corner and she's waiting just for you. Well she's not around the corner and if she were, she's sure as heck not waiting for you. Besides, there's nothing better in Elsinore than me. Take a good look. I'm as hot as it gets around here. And it's about time Hamlet woke up to that fact.

Oh, Hamlet? *(Girlishly)* He's my boyfriend ... He's a Prince. When we get married I'll be a Princess. Princess Ophelia ... Has a nice ring to it. *(Sarcastically)* If I ever see a ring, that is. Up to a few weeks ago, me and Hamlet were really hot and heavy. He couldn't keep his hands off me. Not that I wanted him to. Then his old man ups and dies ... Just like that. He lays down to take a nap in the garden and croaks. Now, all of the sudden, Hamlet doesn't have time for me. He's too busy asking dumb questions and moping around about his dead father and his live-wire mother. Do you know she married Hamlet's uncle before the old king's body was even cold? Well, from what I hear the old man wasn't that hot when he was alive. So, you can't blame Gertrude for goin' for the gusto. A woman has needs ... I can vouch for that.

Hamlet acted all surprised and everything when his mother and Claudius tied the knot. Where has he been? Everybody in Elsinore knew Gertrude and Claudius were an item. And it's not like Hamlet and his old man were that close ... The king wasn't close to anyone. He was the king, for heaven's sakes. But Hamlet and his mother were real close. I mean, like, really close. Like in a spooky sort of way? But still, your old man dies and your mom marries your uncle ... it's got to weird you out a little bit. I get that ... I'm an understanding person. I can see how he's all melancholy and everything. I tried to help him out of his funk. I even suggested we get away for a few days. He's a prince ... It's not like he's got anything he's gotta do. That's the cool part of being a prince. So I said, "Let's get a place at the beach. Or maybe the mountains. Just hang out ... The two of us. We'll take walks ... Drink some wine ... See a play." He's always saying "the play's the thing." You know what he says to me? He said I should get me to a nunnery. A nunnery? Nobody parties at a nunnery. And besides they don't even allow guys. Geez ...

But, like I said, he's got a lot on his mind ... And he's deep. Very deep. I think deep guys are soooo sexy. Don't you? But I wish he'd get off this father hang-up of his. Now, he thinks Claudius, that's the new King — he's Hamlet's uncle and his stepfather. He's also the queen's husband and her brother-in-law. You gotta be some kind of genius to keep all these royal family relationships straight around here. Well, anyway, Hamlet thinks Claudius killed his father ... Hamlet's a big conspiracy buff. But, he doesn't just think it ... He knows it. Said his father told him. I mean, the man's dead ... How's he gonna tell anyone anything? But, get this ... Hamlet says his father's ghost told him. *(Holds her hand up to make a pledge.)* If I'm lyin', I'm dyin'. And get this ... The ghost told Hamlet that Claudius poured some poison in his ear when he was sleeping. I get all creepy just thinking about it. Hamlet thinks he should avenge his father and kill Claudius. If it was anyone else, I'd warn the king to hire an army of food tasters. But this is Hamlet we're talking about. I love him, but the probability of him putting together a plan to kill the king and then actually doing it has two chances ... Slim and none ... And even between those two, Hamlet would have trouble choosing.

My father says I should stay as far away from Hamlet as I can get. He says he's nothing but trouble. But my father says a lot of things ... "To thine own self be true ... Neither a borrower nor a lender be ... " Ya da da. Ya da da. So Hamlet's got a few issues. What guy doesn't? If you're gonna wait for the perfect guy to show up, you'll end up a shriveled old maid. And I intend to get what I want, using what I got while I still got it. I know Hamlet. And I know with a little encouragement and a gentle shove ... My brother, on the other hand, thinks Hamlet is a little light in the leotards, if you get my drift. But he says that about every guy I date. Laertes is such a jerk. Hamlet is not that way. Trust me on that. He's gonna be the king someday. Claudius is gonna shuffle off this mortal coil sooner or later. And then Hamlet will be King and I'll be the queen. Queen Ophelia. People will refer to me as her majesty. Her majesty. Sounds so ... so ... majestic. That'll be great, being the queen ... I can't wait.

When I'm Queen, you'll bow when I walk into a room. You'll stand when I stand. You won't sit until I sit. You'll laugh at all my jokes and call me highness. You'll do what I tell you to do. And when I go back to a reunion with all those girls who teased me in convent school ... Well, they can all line up to kiss my royal ... signet ring. *(A clock chimes offstage.)* Oh, I have to go. Hamlet asked me to meet him in the great hall. I think he's going to propose ... He didn't say that in so many words. Which is odd because when he does say anything it's usually in so many words. I'm not sure what the heck he's talking about. But, I'm sure he's going to ask me to marry him ... *(Rising desperation)* I mean, he has to ask me to marry him. He just has to ... If he doesn't ask me to marry him ... I swear ... I'll kill myself. *(She runs off.)*

Popcorn
by Troy Diana and James Valletti

A young woman from India who has recently moved to Brooklyn, New York, is the victim of a terrifying incident while on a train heading home after work. A stranger in the city frequently defined for newcomers by its crime and violence, the young woman is incapable of action and there are no courageous passengers who unexpectedly rush to her rescue. The incident raises serious questions about tolerance and understanding that demand not conformity but compassion if we are to live in a more inclusive society. This thought-provoking excerpt helps to crystallize the contemporary urban myth of moral decline and the futile search to restore law and order, while at the same time provides very real and valuable lessons about treating each other as equals.

FEMALE: When I first moved to New York from India, I lived in Brooklyn. It was mostly an African American neighborhood. I knew I was different, and there was never a problem with that — until one day when I was on the train heading home. It was late and I had just finished a long day at work. I was falling asleep, when this sharp, quick pain on the side of my face awoke me. Several black teenagers had just slapped popcorn on my face. Then they ran to the next car laughing. I just sat there in shock and pain, with popcorn stuck to my face. At the time, I really didn't know what happened to me, but the pain seemed to be getting worse.

This couple sitting across from me started laughing at me — pointing like I was an animal at the zoo. The man tried to stifle his laughter. He tried to tell his girlfriend to stop laughing, too, but he just couldn't help himself. No one on the train did anything. It was as if nothing wrong happened to me. It made me think something I had never thought before: If I were black, would this have happened?

I was scared to ride the train after that. Six months later I moved to Queens. I do know that things like this don't always happen — I just wish they didn't happen at all.

No Respect
by Bronwyn Barnwell

This provocative monologue bridges a political and social schism that is loaded with issues and messages for all who claim to be civilized and open-minded, even as the world seems to be crumbling around them. An undercurrent of bitterness and hostility lurks just beneath the surface as the character voices a resonant metaphor to underscore the crippling blindness of our collective failure to learn the lessons of the past. Here is a timely reminder of the unrest and disenchantment that stand guard at the barren crossroad between duty and resentment and between irresponsible freedom and responsible compromise — it all depends on the side you choose to take.

EMMA: Wait what? *(Beat)* Back up. *(Beat)* What did you just say? Please repeat that again because I don't think I heard you right because if that is what you just said … *(Beat)*

My god! Are you serious? People who join the Army are dumb? What is wrong with you? How can you say that? How could you possibly say that? You can say the war is dumb, you can say that the Army itself is dumb, but you cannot in any way call the men and women who *fight* in the Army dumb. How can you say that? Because you don't like what they are fighting for? Because you don't believe in the cause? Well good for you. You can disagree with the cause all you want. I don't know if I believe in it myself, but you can in no way belittle the people who are giving their lives for a cause *they* believe in.

24

It's their beliefs, their lives, and you are in no way allowed to judge that because you have your own ideas. You see yourself blowing up buildings later in the name of things you believe in. I don't judge that even though I don't agree with it. I haven't called you dumb for that! You say you have friends who held rallies and blew up buildings against the government. Well, I had babysitters who went off to the Army. I have family in the Army. I have friends who are in the Army. So when you say people who fight in the Army are dumb, you are calling people I love dumb. Just because you don't understand it and you can't wrap your head around the personality and mentality it takes to go into war, doesn't mean you can judge the people that possess it. I would like to see you be thrust into a conservative school in a conservative state, and see how easy it is for you to express your opinions.

You think you are so special because you aren't afraid to speak up about what you believe. Well I hate to break it to you, that's because most people agree with you. I'd like to see you go to Afghanistan, and try to tell me that you wouldn't shoot when you are shot at. That you wouldn't feel the need to kill the man who just shot your friend. You don't know. You *can't* know what that feels like. You call yourself so liberal, so open-minded. You don't deserve to call yourself that. You can't because you are calling people you don't understand, and can't relate to, primitive and stupid. I used to respect you because you are able to speak freely about the way you feel, but now I don't. I have zero respect for you.

Inquest
by G.L. Horton

Elaine, a young mother, skidded off a rain-soaked highway and the car plunged into a river with her children in the backseat. Although she managed to save her daughter, Elaine's son Timmy drowned and she has yet to recover from the pain and guilt of that tragic event. This story is a disquieting tale of heart-wrenching recrimination — Elaine's husband blames her for the accident — and regret that will not allow the bruises to heal or the heart to mend. In this episode, faith and fantasy weave back and forth as Elaine struggles to reconcile a mother's grief with the harsh reality of a child's death … and asks only for permission to heal her wounds.

ELAINE: Yesterday I was cleaning upstairs when I heard the door slam and something slap down on the hall table, just the way Timmy used to dump his books and things when he came in from school. And I forgot, just for a second, that he was dead. I yelled, "Tim, take your stuff to your room!" and he yelled back, "OK, Mom!" and I smiled, and then I realized that he couldn't have, that I was hearing things. But it was so clear and real that I felt an unreasoning hope in my heart, maybe all the rest was what wasn't real, a bad dream, and now at last I'm awake. I went down the stairs, afraid and yet — there, on the hall table, was Timmy's baseball glove.

It wasn't there earlier. It couldn't have been. I keep it upstairs — in my sewing basket. I know that's strange, but I like to have it near me. It's worn from the shape of his hand and it smells like him and when I touch it I can almost feel his presence. Even if I had walked in my sleep and carried it down myself, Frank would have brought it up at breakfast, he makes such a fuss whenever I — I was so happy! Tim was alive! He'd just been hiding, playing this trick on us! Or else Frank hid him away, took him away from me the way he's taken Jennifer, but Tim's got free, he's come back to me!

I started to laugh — and then I got scared. I knew that if Tim left that glove on the table, it wasn't his body that did it. His body was in the coffin. Frank's mother saw it. She wouldn't lie to me. She was at the funeral. She told me what Tim was wearing. She told me he looked at peace. But he's not at peace. He's here. Oh my darling boy, my baby — Tim. What is it? Where does it hurt? Tell Momma, so she can make it better. Oh, tell me — why?

The Blahs

by Shirley King

Amy, a brave young girl barely in her teens, is battling cancer —
and time — with both affection and aggression. She also writes poetry,
skillfully juggling rhythms and rhymes to capture the hope and longing
always lurking beyond the fringe of her serious illness. She has such a
fresh, buoyant, and humorous outlook on life that she emerges as a
mature and understanding young woman — surprising in the strength
of her emotions and the courage of her resolve to loving others first,
even as she may be facing her own death. In coming to terms with
herself and her life, Amy's struggle is inevitably the triumph of a noble
spirit and soul.

AMY: Know how you get the blahs sometimes? That's what my
mom calls it. The blahs. Well, today I'm on my way to get treated for
the blahs again. I was having trouble getting dressed because like, what
should I wear? Nothing looks right, maybe because I've dropped a few
pounds. Okay, more than a few.

Pants and a big sweater so I can hide my ribs sticking out a mile? I
pinned the pants so they wouldn't fall down. Want the funny side?
Losing my pants at the clinic might be wicked cool or well, not even
close. But you know, the doctor might laugh. Even I might laugh.
Prob'ly not Mom. Lately she's serious but trying to hide it. You know
— that cheerful voice that starts to break if she's not careful?

If I've got time I want to be a poet. My English teacher says what I
write are verses but I don't care. They seem like poems to me. I mean
words that rhyme? Sometimes.

Last night I looked up the word "navigate" after my dad said, "Let's
navigate this in the most hopeful way." That's sailor talk because Dad
was in the Navy. Navigate: setting and holding a course like sailors do.
Well, that's sorta what I'm doing. Mom said something about life span.
I don't think I want to go into that.

So anyway, I'm dressed now. Yeah, I know. A cap might look better
and nobody wears a turban except fortune-tellers but, hey, this is what
I like to call stylin'. Before all this, I just wanted to blend in, like the

polar bears in those white-out blizzards on Animal Planet. Well, you can forget that. No way am I blending in now.

My friend Kaitlyn keeps asking, "What's wrong with you?" Well, I've got something I can't even pronounce so I tell her it's a bone marrow problem. I don't say "malignancy" because that sounds way too serious. I keep hoping my hair grows back blonde. I've never been a blonde. Wouldn't that be cool?

So what should I take to the clinic to read? This copy of *Love Story* I found in my mom's bookcase? You know that story? Love means never having to say you're sorry? I don't quite get that. Seems to me saying you're sorry's not such a bad thing when you love someone. Mom keeps saying it when she accidentally drops a dish in the kitchen, like it's something to do with me, and maybe it is. She's really jumpy these days.

I keep telling Mom it's okay, even if some days it's totally not okay. I mean losing my lunch is not so good but that's nobody's fault — right? Mom says she's sorry for that too. Sometimes I wish she could go back to being the mom I used to have, the one who got on my case for having a messy room or not feeding Molly, our beagle, or not finishing my homework. At the time I thought she was being way too harsh. Not now. Now I know she was just being a regular mom.

Okay, gotta go — but first, here's a poem I wrote last night.

> Time is what I hope I have
> While navigating life and all
> And I will do the best I can
> To outspan time and not get small — and disappear.

It doesn't all rhyme? That's okay, I'll work on it. I've got time.

28

Helena

by Glenn Alterman

This dark and chilling original sketch depicts the vivid deterioration of Helena, a defiant and lonely young woman who has repressed the recent death of her mother by retreating into the world of art to escape the net of indifference and hostility in which she has been trapped. The episode is a frightening study of the self-destructive effects of despair and loneliness on a sensitive adolescent who has yet to come to terms with the demons that have shaped her troubled youth. Helena's descent into darkness is a compelling tale of the struggle to find herself in the present when haunted by a past that cannot be understood and must be destroyed in a cold and unforgiving act of self-destruction.

HELENA: Paint, just paint, that's all. That's all I wanted to do. And when Mother died, I finally could. I could paint, full time. Indulge myself. So I started that very morning, right after the funeral. Went out and bought hundreds of canvasses and paint supplies. I started, I began. I loved the smell of the paints, the colors. The pinks, yellows, blues. Started making all kinds of strokes with my brush. First wide, then small. I'd jump up and down and cover a whole canvas! Wild, abstract designs. For the first time in my life I was expressing myself!

I'd cover a canvas, then start another. Rainbows, rivers, anything. I couldn't care less about meals, social engagements. I wanted, no *needed*, to express myself! Browns, oranges, reds! Fill another canvas, then another! Time was melting. Clouds and winds of color were flying across my canvasses. The phone would ring, I wouldn't answer. The door bell, I'd ignore it. I was painting, painting from my soul! One canvas after another! The paint started spilling over me, it felt wonderful!

Then I ... I started rolling around in it, yeah, the paint. The colors covering me. Grays, blues, browns! Soon I became my own canvas. The paint fell on my face, spilled in my ears. I started rolling around in it! I got it in my mouth, my eyes! I couldn't see, no, but I could *feel* the colors, *feel them!* Then I started swallowing it, the paint. Drinking, pouring can after can, can after ... *(She abruptly stops, pauses, looks*

29

around, and then slowly speaks.) I don't remember, have no idea how I ended up here. They told me I'm lucky I'm alive. Lucky I'm not blind. Lucky I used water colors … Mother's death, maybe it was more than … I just wanted to paint, that's all. Express myself. Paint.

A Blue Streak
by Staci Swedeen

In this monologue, originally performed as an evening of independent, stand-alone character sketches titled "Talking With," Missy, a woman of delicate charms but obviously irritable and in despair, imagines she is aging much too quickly. It is a revelation that she can neither credit nor accept, but which drives her to reevaluate her life and what she mistakenly believes may be a crumbling marriage. In desperation she enrolls in an exercise class to confront the ravages of time.

This therapeutic rite of passage provides an intimate glimpse of the trauma Missy is experiencing in the inevitable "aging thing" that she is determined to conquer at all costs, and despite the hardships and struggles it will certainly entail. Her nightmare world of workouts, however, is more comic than serious and offers a nice tongue-in-cheek point of view on exercise in general.

MISSY: I'm not taking this aging thing well. I always thought that I would, that I'd be one of those smiling, super-fit, Jane Fonda clones. Do you have any idea how many funky dance classes you'd have to take to look like that? Do you? But I keep trying because, hey, what's the alternative? Tomorrow's my birthday. I know, thanks, I don't look it. Right. This morning I woke up and I could smell my body rotting. Really, I smelled it. Now, I'm not sick or anything, but I smelled this sweet smell, dank, and it stuck in my throat. I knew that this body that I'm in would one day be — I mean, I felt like I — I'm decomposing. That, in fact, my body is already — already — breaking down, just so subtly that most days I don't notice.

If I keep busy I don't think about it so much. But I lost interest in being in this body, you know what I mean? I just thought, no — no, thank you, I don't want to experience this. Oh, sometimes, sometimes, it's okay — like after aerobics, or eating chocolate, but most of the time … and I don't want Jack to know. I'm afraid that he'll, he'll leave. Wouldn't you? I can't tell him. I don't know how to tell him. So I keep at it, buying new lipstick and taking Tae Bo. How do you say to someone — have you noticed anything recently? That I'm disintegrating? That you're making love to a corpse?

CHAPTER 2
SONGS OF FIRE AND ICE

*"When life does not find a singer to sing her heart,
she produces a philosopher to speak her mind."*
— Khalil Gibran, *The Prophet*

Songs of fire and ice express universal human qualities in a sharp, contemporary voice. Some of the characters sever all connection with human society and remain in brooding loneliness after a failed struggle to achieve personal fulfillment. Other characters spin out complex fantasies in a world of dark self-discovery. All of the characters stumble along life's path and catch fleeting glimpses of their mortality and unexpected moments of grace.

The one common element of these monologues is a "current event" or "recent happening" that calls attention to issues that are at the core of our existence now. The monologues are also a useful tool to enlarge our perception of life and make us aware of the complexities of living daily life in the face of ever-changing conflicts and confrontations. We are witness to the shifting and destructive tides of power and passion, as well as the heroic or rash acts of characters that extend the depth and scope of our capacity to understand and show compassion for others.

These candid character snapshots are evocative in their perceptive observations about human neurosis and antic whimsy. Although the characters are much like us today — familiar human beings expressing universal qualities while at odds with present day social mores, customs, or laws — we must dig deep beneath their superficial exteriors to unearth the hidden seeds of dysfunction and eccentricity that lie within us all and make us all at once alike and yet different.

Walking a fine line between childlike fantasy and harsh reality, the courageous characters attempt to confront the private demons that haunt them. Warmhearted and quirky comic characters travel the road not taken, but find themselves drawn into a series of unfortunate misadventures. Prickly and treacherous characters who know one another's secrets, and are destined to betray them, try to balance the tension between resentment, chaos, and frustration by evading the sober truth that there are no clear and simple answers to life's unexpected detours.

Some of the characters may be seen as "misfits" or "outlaws" suffering from periodic emotional or psychological dilemmas that have resulted in low self-esteem, loss of human dignity, extended periods of isolation, or withdrawal from society. Invariably, however, they expose their secret, private feelings and gradually discover a more genuine understanding of the infirmities and misfortunes that human beings must endure if we are to truly know ourselves ... and our purpose in life.

We also hear strident urban voices of characters that, amid the hurt or even the hilarity, gain a healthy dose of self-confidence to help them weather stormy disappointments and begin sunny new lives with a renewed sense of purpose. These imaginative and engrossing voices are a collage of authentic, personal narratives that depict the discouragement, derision, and disbelief to which the characters are too often subjected. But as the characters probe into their often self-destructive or disillusioned lives, they also discover new truths about themselves and the world in which they live — though, perhaps, not the "happy ending" they, or we, had hoped for them.

The songs of fire and ice characters are lyrical hymns to those who are at a loss for direction and desperate for a sense of meaning and fulfillment. In other words, they are all of us some of the time and some of us all the time. They sing the songs of those who are frequently obliged to hide behind the mask of anonymity in order to stake a personal claim on their own lives. Gentle humor and tender moments of poignancy are blended as the characters embrace a greater truth: The need to stop destroying themselves and to destroy, instead, the unforgiving demons that have kept them all prisoners ... powerless to pursue their own destiny.

Role Playing

A good starting point in playing these roles is to depict characters that are flesh and blood, who express themselves in simple thoughts, and respond in natural and spontaneous actions. There is a flavor and texture of directness in the characters that at times suggests a "raw slice of life," so your audition performance may need to be more restrained and subtle to help communicate a character's attitude or mood. Movement may also be less fluid or graceful than traditional audition practice demands.

Be aware of the need to be easily heard and understood, with adequate rate and volume to meet the demands of each character's action described in the text. Subtleties of *pausing* and *phrasing* may also play an important role in voicing dialogue to suggest different temperaments and emotional or mental states of mind. Although there may be moments of comic intent in some of the monologues or duo scenes, they are usually incidental to character development so you will need to practice restraint and refrain from excessive exaggeration to underline the comic potential of the characters at the expense of the seriousness of the situation.

Remember that stage figures in contemporary theatre are very much like us today, so look for the larger personal truths just beneath the surface of the dialogue and translate those discoveries into appropriate gestures and physical actions that reinforce your character portraits. You may wish to chart believable physical changes that will take place during the audition as well. Do make sure, however, that your character portraits are truly distinctive and individual in attention to detail as well as in subtle nuance.

The Lady with All the Answers
By David Rambo

Eppie, a mature and shrewd advice columnist for a major newspaper syndicate (read Ann Landers), is razor-sharp in her observations of human nature as she tries to comfort a world normally glimpsed in tabloids without any hint of pretense or sentimentality. The raw emotions boiling underneath her words, however, provide such biting humor and popular culture literacy that we are ravenous for more! Seated at her desk surrounded by piles of neatly stacked letters, Eppie randomly selects one and begins to compose aloud an imaginary response to the writer's classical question, "What is the proper way to hang the toilet paper in the bathroom?"

EPPIE: *(Reading aloud)* "Dear Ann Landers: While I was visiting family back in Sioux City, I brought up the subject of how they all needed to reverse their paper towels and toilet paper on the spools since they were placed incorrectly. The paper should be coming from the wall up toward the top, over and out. They all disagreed. Please settle this for us. Signed, 'Paper Crazy.'"

Now, first of all, you come into my home as a guest — relative or not — and tell me how to hang my toilet paper ... bub, the elevator going down has your name on it.

Be that as it may, I wrote "Paper Crazy" that there was no right or wrong way to hang it, but my preference is the same as his relatives', back against the wall.

And that's how sixty million people found out how Ann Landers hangs her toilet paper. *(Pause. She finds this next statement almost incredible.)* Fifteen thousand letters came in. Fifteen thousand letters! About *toilet paper!*

It just boggles the mind. *(The letter goes back in the file.)* With all the important issues that divide our country — war, morality, abortion, guns, and nuclear proliferation — apparently, this is one of the most polarizing issues of the day. Well, let's see if it's still true. *(Directly to the audience, looking for a show of hands.)* Who thinks it should hang down in the back, against the wall? How many of you? I'm not asking how it's hung in your house; I'm asking how you *think* it should be hung. Who's for back against the wall? *(She coaxes the response. Then —)* All right. And how many think it should go the other way, come up from behind and hang down in front? *(She coaxes the response. Then —)*

All right. Now, let's see how many of you live in a household where there is some disagreement on the issue — the issue of tissue? *(She takes in the response.)* And who's ever gone into someone else's bathroom, taken the roll off the wall, and switched it around? *(To those who respond affirmatively —)* Tsk, tsk, tsk ...

Now about whether the seat should be left up or down — No, I've got work to do. Besides, the answer to that one's nonnegotiable. Right, ladies? *(Back to work.)*

The Whispers of Saints
By Mark Scharf

In this complex monologue, Laura, a mature but manic woman reeling from a sense of betrayal, despair, and an unexpectedly sudden divorce, struggles to overcome a gnawing mood of loneliness and despair by retreating to her mother's beach house to lament the abrupt passing of better times. On the verge of an emotional breakdown, and consumed by lingering depression and a rage for revenge, Laura finally opens up to her mother's much younger lover and shares the self-inflicted wounds of her life that have crippled a fight for survival. Laura's baffling and ultimately terrifying confessions unleash a flood of painful memories, somber regrets, and senseless missteps as she reflects on the meaning of her life.

LAURA: I never used to be able to understand how anyone who was ever in love could hurt the other person. I thought, no matter what someone did, no matter what happened, if you ever loved that person — really loved them — then how could you bring yourself to hurt them? I'd read these stories in the newspapers, you know? Heard them on the TV about some woman or some guy shooting their ex to death — sometimes right in front of their children. And I could not understand that. It was just so far beyond anything I could imagine feeling about someone. To do something like that ... they'd have to be a monster. *(She slams a shell onto the table.)*

But now ... Now I understand it. What those people were thinking — or maybe it's what they weren't thinking. I understand what they were feeling. How bad they hurt inside ... they'd do anything to make it stop. Anything ... I don't know if it's so much hate as looking for some way to make the pain stop. Make it stop permanently. *(She gets up from the table and paces.)*

I know what it is to hate now, you know? I prayed every morning for a month for that man to die. To get some disease, some cancer to slowly eat away at him until he was dead. So he would die alone. Like he'd left me. Alone. But then I got kind of scared about doing that. Like maybe instead of him getting cancer I'd come down with something because I wished it for him.

Do you follow me? So, I stopped praying for him to die. I stopped praying at all, actually. I mean compared to what goes on in the world what happened to me was nothing, you know? *Nothing.* I mean, what is my marriage compared to mass murder or children stepping on land mines or — whatever. Take your pick. I was carrying around this incredible ball of pain pressing on my heart and stomach. *(Small pause.)*

And then I understood how someone could take a gun and track down the one who was causing this pain — find that person and just end it. Because then I wouldn't have to worry about it anymore. I wouldn't have to think about what he was doing or why — because then it wouldn't matter. *(Small pause.)*

Do you think that makes me a monster?

Blind Spots
by Colette Freedman

In this character portrait, Kate, a selfish, self-consumed, and frustrated woman, continues to have a turbulent relationship with her younger sister, Gretchen. Here she struggles with a sense of guilt as she relives a childhood incident in which she failed to save her sister from a tragic mishap. Her self-portrait is etched in shades of gray as the lines between real and imagined become more blurred. But it is obvious that Kate's will to live is stronger than her desire for self-sacrifice.

KATE: Dad had gotten me that coat. The pink one, with the white buttons. I had wanted it for so long. She always sewed everything, remember? My fashion statement was a bolt of cloth from Jo-Ann Fabric and Mom's skills with a needle. I never had anything new. Anything special. And I wanted that coat so badly. Everyday, I used to pass Winkies and it was there in the window on a mannequin with a long braid. I wanted to be that mannequin so badly ... just so I could wear that pink coat. And finally I went to Dad and begged him. I knew Mom would think it was wasteful, unnecessary ... uppity. But Dad ... You may have had him wrapped around your little finger, but when I explained why I wanted that coat ... why I needed that coat. He understood. He actually listened. It may have been the first and the last time that Dad ever heard anything I said, but the next week ... that coat was under the Christmas tree. Right next to your skates. *(Her anger has turned to distress and tears start to run down her cheek.)* Dad had given me that coat. I couldn't get it wet. I didn't want to get it wet. I didn't want to ruin it. I was afraid ... I was so afraid he wouldn't love me any more. *(Realizes.)* I didn't even try to save you.

Greensboro: A Requiem
by Emily Mann

Survivors of a 1979 massacre of racially mixed, unarmed demonstrators in the small town of Greensboro, North Carolina, by the Ku Klux Klan together with the American Nazi Party and with the help of the local police assisted by the F.B.I., now recall the incident in a series of haunting interviews. Although fourteen people were gunned down (five were killed, nine injured) *in a caravan drive-by attack — and the assault was captured on film — repeated trials in Greensboro brought only acquittals for the men responsible. In this interview, Floris Cauce Weston, iron-willed but subdued widow of Cesar Cauce, voices her own requiem on the lingering grief and sorrow that offers an insightful glimpse of death, loss, and healing.*

FLORIS: I guess I haven't dealt with a lot of anger. I'm the only one of the survivors, I think, who stopped doing any social justice work, any political work at all. I feel guilty I didn't spend full-time on my own case. I'm really grateful to Marty and Dale and Signe, the other widows, that they followed through with that process, due process. It was very important, but I couldn't stay through to the end. The widows and Nelson helped the lawyers uncover the full extent of the conspiracy, the role of the government and the police. See — there were police people who really knew a lot. The murder had the character of an accident, but someone let it happen.

I became firmly convinced it was preventable. But I didn't know where to place my anger. See, I could always understand the Klan's point of view. They have always identified who they hate. They have always admitted they're violent people. I suppose I'm most angry at the police. In my eyes, they were on trial more than the Klan. And I'm angry at us for letting it happen. Even though we didn't mean to. But we were fighting armed men with ideas, with words.

I don't know ... I guess, Greensboro was a place where I lost my purpose in life. I still don't go to demonstrations. I don't think they work. I don't know if they ever did. I think what really gets done gets done someplace else. If social change is going to be accomplished, it's going to be done in offices, I don't know. I was twenty-four years old when this happened. I thought I was doing the right thing. I went straight out of college into a social movement ... I didn't have the skills necessary to interpret this. Cesar ... I don't know. Talking helps. I try to put a piece of the puzzle together every day. And I'm quiet. I guess that's what they wanted. It's fifteen years later, and I'm still quiet.

The Parables of Bo Peep
By Cassie Silva

In this charmingly original, quirky, and fractured fairy tale satire, an insecure Little Bo Peep of nursery rhyme fame is all grown up ... but isn't looking so "little" these days! Wearing a housecoat and slippers over a frock and apron, Little Bo Peep takes us on a madcap romp through our favorite children's stories, and no one escapes her antic rant as she recounts her uproarious misadventures with mile-a-minute action, nonstop laughter, and a warmhearted moral to point out what fools we mortals can be. Unlike the classic tale, however, all does not end happily for Little Bo Peep, proving once again that the more things change the more they really remain the same — just a new beat on an old drum. Is Little Bo Peep's self-image entirely accurate, or is fairytale society to blame?

LITTLE BO PEEP: *(Stands with her head cocked to one side, looking out to audience as if she is looking at herself in a mirror.)* Well, good morning, foxy lady. *(Tosses hair.)* Bo Peep, you look fine today. Have you been working out? *(Pause)* Yea, I can tell. You look like you've lost ten pounds since I saw you last! No really! *(She swaggers*

39

over to the scale and steps on, looking confident. She glances down at the number and freezes.)
　Stop! (She steps off the scale moodily and kicks it.) I am a heifer! Gretel can eat an entire gingerbread house and not gain an ounce. What is wrong with me? Why can't I just prick my finger on a sewing machine and fall asleep for ten years, bypass that whole inconvenient "having to eat" thing, and wake up hot and skinny? It's like I'm Alice, wandering through Wonderland, and everything I see has a little sign on it crying, "Eat Me. Eat Me. *Eat Me!*" Mother Goose is no help. "You just need to take better care of yourself. Your friend Rapunzel's hair is soooo pretty. Why don't you ask her what conditioner she uses?" *(Sarcastically)* Thanks Mother! If Rapunzel locked herself away in a tower would you want me to as well? *(Sighs.)* My curls are lackluster, my frock is stretched at the seams, and I smell like a barnyard. No wonder Jack Horner would rather sit in the corner than ask me to dance at homecoming. Who would want to be seen with me? I don't even want to be seen with me and I am me.
　My friend Jill says I'm one of the prettiest girls she knows, but nobody takes what Jill says too seriously since she got that nasty head injury tumbling down the hill, poor thing. If only boys were more like sheep. Sheep love you unconditionally. Maybe it's time to cast aside my dreams and become one of those crazy cat ladies … only with sheep instead of cats. I'll start naming them after all the boys I've ever loved but who never loved me back. Jack! You come down off that cliff immediately! Peter, you head-butt me one more time and I'll saw off your horns! *(Laughs maniacally to herself and then begins to sing.)* "Little Boy Blue, come blow your horn. The sheep's in the meadow, the cow's in the corn." Where's the boy who looks after the sheep? Standing me up for a date, that darn little creep. *(Clears throat.)*
　It's not that my other friends don't try to help. Beauty told me looks aren't that important, but that's easy for her to say. "Appearances don't matter. What matters is what's in your heart." Yea, unless you're the girl. Little Miss Muffet offered some diet tips, but curds and whey made me bloat up like a water balloon. A lactose intolerant shepherdess; no wonder I'm single. Snow White was kind enough to lend me her magic mirror as a little pick-me-up to boost my self-esteem. "Oh, he's such a charmer. It's impossible not to just burst with confidence when you're

40

told you're the fairest in the land every single morning." *(Glumly)* She wrapped the mirror and left him in my locker while I was in math class. I took him home, hung him on the wall, pulled the cover off ... and he screamed.

Luckily some gifts are returnable. *(Pulls out a book.)* At least Cinderella gave me a present that's bound to be useful: "He's Just Not That Into You" — AKA My Life Story. Well gentlemen, there'll be no more pulling the wool over Bo Peep's eyes! Cinderella claims my Prince Charming is trying to find me, he's just lost, and too stubborn to ask for directions. I used to believe that fairy tale, but after years of waiting, I've come to the conclusion he's probably been hit by a bus. Maybe I'm better off. Sometimes I wish I had a magic ring, or lamp, or any object really, that promised to grant a heartfelt wish. I wouldn't even need three.

I know what you're thinking ... You think I'd wish to be beautiful. Well, you're partially right. I'd wish that everyone else thought I was beautiful ... just the way I am. And even though it would admittedly create more competition, I wish all the other girls would see how beautiful they really are too. It seems like every girl has her own personal dragons to slay, whether she's shut up in a tower waiting for true love's first kiss, or in a cottage in the woods escaping her wicked stepmother. If you're not pretty enough, no one cares whether you exist or not. Where there be dragons, we're all locked away. The sad part is, we spend our whole lives waiting for someone else to show up and rescue us, when the truth is ... we can unlock the door and walk out of that tower at any point. We're just not brave enough to do it alone.

> *(She begins to sing.)*
> Little Bo Peep fell fast asleep,
> And dreamt she was so pretty.
> When she awoke, the mirror it spoke,
> "Dream on," he said with pity.
> "You're ugly as sin, you'll never be thin.
> Why do you even try to fit in?"
> She heaved a sigh, and wiped her eye.
> And then Bo Peep sat down to cry.
> *(BO PEEP stares at her reflection with tears in her eyes.)*

41

Chance Light Snow
by Jolene Goldenthal

A disillusioned and distracted young mother sits quietly in the middle of the floor in an empty room. Near her is a small bundle of children's clothing that she absentmindedly, almost mechanically, picks up, caresses, folds, unfolds, and then folds again. In this absorbing account of a recent dream — real or imagined — the young mother travels down a dark path of half-truths and self-delusion that helps to illuminate her lingering trauma and its cruel aftermath. All the while we are left to wonder if some "dreams" might just come crashing into our own lives, blazing out of control and distorting reality.

YOUNG MOTHER: I dreamt about a woman who ... drowned her children. Her husband left her ... she didn't know what to do. *(Pause)* She bundled them up in their good warm jackets so they wouldn't be cold ... and she put them in the car ... and she drove to the pond.

It was snowing. Pretty white stuff coming down and down. She thought it would melt ... but it kept coming faster ... and faster ... and faster ...

She got out of the car to look at the snow. And the car ... the car ... went into the pond. The children were crying and then it was quiet. She saw Robbie's red shoulder and Danny's blue arm. She called out to them.

"Robbie!" she called. "Danny! Mommy's here! Mommy's here!"

But it was quiet. *(Pause)* Bad boys. They heard. But they didn't make a sound. Not ... a sound ... *(Pause)* Bad boys. *(Pause)*

I was a child once. My mother took care of me. Washed me. Dressed me. Fed me. Poor Mommy. How did she do that? How did she do that every day? All alone ... only the children. No one to love. No one to laugh with. No one to be pretty for ... *(Absently she picks up something from the heap of clothing, puts it down.)* Do you hear them? Crying? I thought I heard ... something. It's the snow maybe. It's still snowing ... And my dream. My terrible dream. *(Pause)* Where is he? Why did he leave us? Where did he go? *(Long pause)*

I cried. The children cried. I cried because he left. They cried because I cried. And they were hungry. Poor babies.

I sat on the floor and I played with them. I sang for them. I clapped my hands and I sang for them and I told them it was a party.

"Clap your hands! Sing a song! It's a party!" I said. But they were hungry. They cried and cried. I didn't know what to do. *(Pause)*

I put on their jackets and went for a ride. *(Long pause)* It started to snow. Pretty white snow. I wanted to show them the pretty white snow. *(Abruptly she snatches a piece of small clothing from the bundle and slowly begins to tear it into small strips.)*

He told me he loved me. He told me! *He* told me he'd be with me always. And then he … he went away. He went away and he never came back. I wanted to hurt him. *(She rises suddenly, dropping the torn bits of fabric to the floor.)* He'll be sorry, won't he? He'll be sorry. But it's too late. I'll tell him! I'll tell him! It's too late. *(Long pause)* And it's all your fault.

I went to the pond. It was snowing … *(She glances desperately at the stark and empty room.)* I went to the pond. *(Pause)* I went to the pond … *I wanted to hurt you! I wanted to punish you!* They're gone … And it's all your fault …

Lives of the Great Waitresses
by Nina Shengold

In these two zippy, crisp comic character portraits we catch a fleeting glimpse of the lives of two winning waitresses, Kay and Melissa, captured in tabloid-like flashes of well armed nips-and-tucks at a "greasy spoon" diner. Kay, a mature, born-again African American woman, offers a thoughtful observation on a poignant incident that set her new life in motion and on a path of righteousness. Melissa, a younger and novice waitress in her first day of work, is an unlikely counter cohort with a social conscience marked by an optimism for life that is full of love and wonder.

KAY: You either got it, or you don't. If you don't, you won't ever. So don't even bother. Don't strain. Oh, there's things you can learn, sure. The fine points. The stance. "Heat that up for you?" "Toasted?" But honey — scratch that, make it hon — a truly great waitress is *born*.

You get what I mean? It's a feel thing. Deep under the bones of your bones. In your cells. Some reporter once asked Louis Armstrong what "swing" meant. Louis looked the guy dead in the eyeball and said, "If you gotta ask, you'll never know." He would've made a great waitress.

My very first diner, we had one. Flo Kelly. A goddess in Supp-Hose. Flo was all waitress. She could fill two dozen shakers one-handed and never spill one grain of salt. She could carry eight Hungry Man specials lined up on her arm like a charm bracelet. Flo could serve pie á la mode so it looked like Mount Everest topping the clouds. She poured gravy like tropical rain. In Flo's maraschino-nailed fingers, the short-order carousel spun like the Wheel of Fortune, and never, not once, did a customer's coffee get cold.

Well, I mean to tell you, that diner was *hers*. If Jesus Himself Amen came in and sat down to supper, he would've tipped double. Then one Blue-Plate Special, right after the lunch rush, Flo hung up her hairnet, cashed in her checks, and went sunny-side up. And that's when the Lord took my order. I knew what I was. I was called. *(She steps closer.)*

Look in my eyes. I know mysteries way beyond menus. I have felt the Lord's love pierce my heart like a skewer through gyros. I have seen Jesus weep ice-kold milk with a K. *(She holds out her hand.)*

Heat that up for you? Hon?

MELISSA: This is my first day of work. Not here. Ever. My family had money and nobody made me. I came to this city to look for a job and nobody would hire me. It's kind of like being a virgin — I'm not any more, but I was once, you know? — and I'm telling you, nobody wants to be first. Too much pressure. My roommate said, "Lie." So I did. *(She sits.)*

People think if you haven't done something before, you're an idiot. People can't know what's inside you. You don't know yourself till you're given a chance. Then all of a sudden this new personality starts to swell under your skin, bursting through where you'd never expect it, and nothing you thought you were makes any sense. You're elastic.

You're putty. You've been up for hours, making love to a man whose back ripples with muscles you've never felt, feeling your body expand and explode and dissolve into air, into something like stars, and it doesn't seem possible that you could open your eyes to the same old alarm clock and fit in the same pair of shoes.

I don't want to lose this. This newness, this urgent, sharp knowledge that everything matters. That being good matters.

I want to do everything well.

I know, I'm a waitress. It's not what I've dreamed of, what anyone dreams of, but I can make a difference. I do. There are lives on each stool at that counter. The old man who's ordered his Sanka and Shredded Wheat every morning for twenty-five years. *(She nods towards someone in the audience.)* Otto.

The woman who fought with her husband last night and treated herself to French toast with her friend who just had a mastectomy. Velma and Ruth. The man who panhandled the price of his coffee. Muhammed.

I touch them. I give them the quiet sensation that once in their sad, uncontrollable lives, they wanted a small thing and got it. I brought it. I bore them a gift. And that matters. *(She hangs up her apron.)*

You watch me. I'm going to be brilliant. I'm going to be one of the greats.

Freedom High
by Adam Kraar

Roz, a courageous young African American civil rights worker is training student volunteers on a college campus in Ohio to go to Mississippi in 1964 to help register other African Americans to vote. She offers a panoramic view of oppressed men and women struggling to achieve their rights and calls attention to the injustices of the past by taking a chilling look at the events that have since shaped African American history and brought national attention to the on-going civil rights movement. In this original monologue, Roz reveals her initial fears by reminding herself of the ideals that have kept her going and that the movement foreshadows cataclysmic social change just around the corner. Although doubtful, she is determined to play an active role in the civil rights movement and to carve out a society in which equality and justice can be born anew ... for all.

ROZ: It's happening, it's really happening.
The good questions, the necessary doubts.
The barriers come up, are shared, and then start to come down.
The Beloved Community.

We will shine our lights
Into Mississippi nights
Until they turn to day.
It is the muddy, bloody, necessary journey.
In the end, we'll all join hands and sing.
We will. We will. We will.
Even Senator Eastland, and Governor Johnson.
Even the Grand Klux ...
I know. I know.
The Grand Klux won't hold my black hand.
Won't join our circle.
And my husband? Linwood?
Will you live to see it?
(Beat)

Where are you, Linwood?
Are you alive?
I wish you were here!
You might laugh at these kids,
But you couldn't hate them.
They would love you, and cry for you,
And want to give you their lives.
Are you with the three that ... disappeared?
I hope, I pray, I beg you, Lord
Let him be alright.
Don't let them ... smash ...
His beautiful, powerful, stubborn head.

The Beloved Community.
We will, we are, we are making
The Beloved Community.

When It Rains Gasoline
by Jason D. Martin

In this original character portrait, Emily, a quite lovely and sensitive — but naïve — high school cheerleader, is the role model type of popular young girl that other adolescents often dream of becoming: teen royalty. Her social world has been filled with magical moments of admiration and celebration in which the boundaries between illusion and fantasy were never clearly drawn. Now she must confront the harsh reality and collateral damage that will surely surface if her "dark secret" is ever revealed. Emily's emotional journey is a story of the choices framed by circumstance that force us, at last, to reveal our true selves even as our make-believe world begins to collapse around us.

EMILY: Sometimes I just wish the world was full of pink bunny rabbits. There would be a beautiful lush forest, green grass, a sparkling brook, and it would always be warm. And all that would live there would be pink bunny rabbits. Hundreds of pink bunny rabbits. They would eat the grass and the leaves and there wouldn't be any wolves to hurt them. Every rabbit's Mom and Dad would love them no matter what … And all the rabbits would be in love … They would all have the perfect mate that would never ever hurt them in any way. They would all be able to trust each other and know that if something bad happened, no one would run away. I know it's a weird dream, but I've heard weirder. My boyfriend used to tell me how cool it would be if there were one-way mirrors into the girl's locker room. That's kind of strange. Then again, he is a guy. I had another friend who thought that rocks were alive and that if you touched them the grease on your fingers would kill them. A little weirder. Someone once told me that he had a premonition that one day we would all have flying waffles for cars. That almost takes the cake for weirdness.

No, I'll tell you the weirdest thing I ever heard was when my doctor told me that I was pregnant ... There is no doubt that that's the weirdest thing I've ever heard. I never knew a fifteen-year-old girl would ... Well, I suppose I've heard about it happening. I guess I never thought it could happen to me. I wish the world were full of pink bunny rabbits.

Lost and Found
by Dori Appel

Torie, an inquisitive young graduate student in her early twenties, has been interviewing three middle-aged homemakers about generational changes in women's lives as part of a research project, and, intentionally or not, finds herself coming to terms with past emotional events with her mother, who suffered a severe breakdown while Torie was in high school. In this candid episode, Torie vividly recalls an incident that shattered her childhood dreams and tries to find something in the event to sustain her in the search for unattainable answers. Although now at a crossroad in her young life, Torie is the one who may have learned the most from her mother, not only about burdens too onerous to bear ... but also about the redemptive power of forgiveness as well.

TORIE: I was only there for the prelude — a little kitchen melodrama. I came home from school and there she was, charging around the kitchen at full tilt, throwing all her baking equipment into cardboard boxes — and believe me, she had equipment! When she saw me she took these two cookie sheets she was holding and clanged them together like cymbals.

"Ta Da! Guess what day this is!"

I just stood there, not knowing what to think, because my mom — most of the time she was a really funny, lively person.

"Independence Day!" she shouted, and threw the cookie sheets on top of a bunch of cake pans. She was grabbing things right, left, and sideways — pie tins, mixing bowls, spoons, spatulas — all that stainless steel clanging and ringing as one more piece hit the pile.

I said, "Mom, what are you doing?" but she was banging open drawers and cabinets, and by this time she was cursing at everything

48

and laughing at the same time, and she really looked pretty crazy. She'd gathered up all her measuring cups — stainless and Pyrex and even some plastic — and she threw them all on the floor and yelled out, "The measure of my days!" A Pyrex one broke when she threw it, and she started picking up the pieces and cut herself, so now she was bleeding on top of everything else, and she'd stopped laughing and was crying and muttering, and then suddenly she yanked a plug out of the wall and knocked her shiny Kitchenaid mixmaster over on its side. It just lay there on the counter like a wrecked car or something while she shouted and beat it with its own electric cord.

I was getting pretty scared — I'd seen her upset and crying before, but this was something else, this was like something out of "I Love Lucy" — except it wasn't funny. It was very serious and scary and I was just wishing that my dad would come home and calm her down. But it was the middle of the afternoon. So I knew that wasn't going to happen, and I couldn't phone him because I was afraid to leave her alone. Finally, she stopped crying and yelling, and she closed up the boxes, and I helped her load them into the car. I wanted to go with her, I said she'd need me to carry things when she got to the Goodwill, but she wouldn't let me. I did get her to come back in the kitchen to put a Band-Aid on her hand, and that's when she saw this little stainless steel quarter cup measure on the floor. She picked it up and washed it very carefully, then dried it with a clean dish towel, and put it back in the drawer. She was leaning against the counter, looking so unbelievably tired. I said I'd make her a cup of tea — the kettle was still sitting on the stove — but she just shook her head and pulled me over to her.

"Torie, honey," she said, "promise me you'll find a better way to measure your days." Then she gave me a quick kiss, grabbed her sweater off the hook, and drove off. *(Beat)* The rest happened in a motel, and she called the front desk within a few minutes, so the medics got there right away. *(Beat.)*

A few months later I found a copy of the hospital report in my dad's desk. It called what she'd done a "suicide gesture," which made me think of a shadow play, or something from a ballet. I imagined this silhouette of my mother tilting her head back as her arm floated up very slowly and tipped a bottle just above her mouth. Only a gesture. Nothing to do with death.

The Subway
by John Augustine

In this inspired comic romp, an effervescent, upbeat, and slightly savory real estate agent pitches all the properties she has available in her New York City portfolio to a group of dazed, unexpectedly trapped subway riders during rush hour. She conjures up a frenzied sense of anticipation and excitement with a burst of lethal laughter in a cold-blooded, ghoulish description of grotesque treasures ready and waiting. The winsome agent sparkles in a scathing, irreverent indictment of the worst aspects of the art of salesmanship. But the good-natured fun and sharply pointed satire also reveals a gem of truth worth the wait for our bankrupt times: "Let the Buyer Beware!"

REAL ESTATE WOMAN: May I have your attention please? I do not rob. I do not steal. I'm in *real estate*. And I have a lovely apartment listed on the upper west side. It has an eat-in kitchen and lovely pre-war features, although it is a modern building. It has several closets that *could* be knocked down to create the *feeling* of space. It doesn't have a doorman, but there is room for one. You don't see many door women. Why is that I wonder? Ladies! Perk up your ears. I just created more job opportunities for us. Now then. The main room can be used as a living room or a bedroom. It's very versatile. I think it would be a lovely meditation room because it is so *won*derfully dark. There is one small window, but you could easily board that up with a bookcase. Or ... for those of you who are not day sleepers, you could easily install several very large picture windows with board approval. God knows what you'd look at. Crack dealers welcome! In fact, I have some good crack for sale right now. Just kidding. That's my sense of humor. Isn't it good? So if everybody would gather by the far door, we can all get off at the next stop and I'll be conducting a walking tour of the upper west side. Bring your check books!

The Stronger Bond
by Kristine McGovern

Two sisters, each in search of personal happiness and meaning in their lives, find themselves on an emotional pilgrimage as they confront the reality of their alcoholic mother's agonizing death. Lucy, the younger sister, is content to be a bookworm and subject to jealous outbursts intended to deride her older sister rather than admit she is as much a victim of her own nature. Adele, the older sister, quietly deals with her own pain and is sweet-spirited in following her true feelings. More than anything else, Adele hopes her family is somehow restored and a renewed sense of mutual respect and dependence may yet arise from the bitter ashes of her mother's death.

The duo scene is an emotional unraveling of old hurts and wounds as well as the mending of a very fragile new beginning for the sisters. The conflict — if not the basic jealousy — of the sisters explores the human relationship between them, and as tensions mount, disquieting truths are invariably put aside to reveal caring, vulnerable human beings who sense each other's anguish and are slowly drawn closer together again. What emerges is a sense of deeper understanding and mutual respect as the sisters see how petty and ugly we can be if we look only at ourselves when we should remember to look at others first — especially those we love — to form the stronger, more lasting, bond.

(Lights come up on LUCY, sitting barefoot on her bed with knees drawn up, writing in a notebook propped on her thighs. Lucy reads aloud as she writes, but the pace is not overly slow. Lucy is a facile thinker and writer.)

LUCY: Dear Mim. I call you Mim because, first of all, that's your name. And second you have never been a mom. You have been a zom, as in zombie, but not a mom or mombie. I find it interesting that your name is Mim, as if your own Mombie knew you would never achieve the circular, encompassing "O" needed to make an m-o-m but would always and forever be stuck with the "I" of m-i-m. It has always been the "I" for you, hasn't it, Mim? It's all about the "I" and the ego, which is the hallmark of the alcoholic, so that's

no surprise. What is surprising — *(A knock at the door. LUCY closes her notebook and tucks it away.)*

ADELE: *(Off-stage)* Lucy?

LUCY: *(Folding herself into a cross-legged position on the bed)* The door's open. *(ADELE enters in a rush.)*

ADELE: Dad just called. The priest is there and they've decided to take Mom off the ventilator. *(LUCY nods.)* They'll wait for us, but we need to leave soon. Right away. Get your shoes and let's go. *(She turns and is heading out the door.)*

LUCY: I'm not going.

ADELE: *(Wheeling toward LUCY)* What?

LUCY: She's in a coma, Adele. She won't know if I'm there or not. Just like she's never known I'm there.

ADELE: Let's not go into that now. She's your mother, and she's dying. We need to say good-bye.

LUCY: I said good-bye to her a long time ago. I don't need to say good-bye to that pathetic bag of bones.

ADELE: Lucy!

LUCY: That's all she is, the poor little thing. A bundle of tiny bones offered up to the Great God Vodka. *(She salaams on the bed.)* Hail, O great god Wod-tka! *(She straightens.)* You know what vodka's made from, don't you? Potatoes! Potatoes killed our Mim. Killed by Mr. Potato-Head. *(She salaams again.)* O, Hail, great Potato-Head!

ADELE: Cut it out, Lucy, and get your shoes. We've got to hurry.

LUCY: I told you I'm not going. Go without me. Give her my best. That's more than she ever gave me.

ADELE: *(Crosses and sits down on the bed, pushing stuffed animals out of the way. She picks up one of the animals.)* She did the best she could, Lucy. She's sick. You know that. You know it's a disease. She couldn't help it.

LUCY: She loved potatoes more than she loved us.

ADELE: She loved us as much as she could.

LUCY: Yeah. She really loved us when she wouldn't consider the liver transplant. All she had to do was quit drinking for six months and they'd give her a new liver. Liv-er. Get it? An organ that lets you live? But that'd mean giving up her precious potato juice. She chose potatoes over us.

ADELE: None of that matters now. She's our mother, she's dying, and we have to say good-bye to her. Now.

LUCY: How can you keep saying, "She's our mother. She's our mother"? She was never a mother. You were the mother. Who fixed breakfast when she was passed out from the night before? Who took me to my first day of school. Let's see ... You're two years older, so you must have been about eight. A little eight-year-old talking to the teacher, filling out the forms. How unreal is that? You're still the mother.

ADELE: I help out, Lucy, that's all. When Dad's out of town, I help out.

LUCY: Good old Dad. Let's not forget about him. God forbid he ever take away her precious bobbies. Bobbies! Who calls bottles "bobbies" anyway? Such a cute little baby with her bobby of potato juice. *(Mimicking Mim)* "Where's my bobby? I want my bobby!" *(Mimicking Dad)* "Here it is, baby. Have a bobby and shut up." He's as sick as she is, you know. Oh, learned all about it at Alateen. And we're probably alcoholics, too —

ADELE: Don't say that! Don't even think that!

LUCY: Why not? There's a genetic predisposition. You know that. We're lucky we didn't end up with fetal alcohol syndrome. Who knows? We probably have it and don't know it.

ADELE: It's nothing to joke about!

LUCY: I'm not joking! *(They glare at each other.)*

ADELE: Lucy, look. I know she hasn't been the best mother —

LUCY: She poured my childhood down the drain! How do I get that back? If it weren't for books, and you ... And my friends. It's amazing I have any friends. How many times have I had any of them over? Two times? Three? Do you know how embarrassing it is when you're afraid your drunken mother will collapse in a puddle or tear off her clothes or scream demented things at them?

ADELE: Yes, I do. *(She's silent a moment.)* I can't argue with you, Lucy. I don't blame you for your feelings. No one would. I just don't want you to blame yourself later on.

LUCY: Why would I do that?

ADELE: Because you had a chance to do the right thing, and you didn't. You didn't say good-bye to your mother. You weren't with her when she was dying.

LUCY: She's in a co-ma, Adele! She won't know if I'm there or not!

ADELE: How do you know? How does anyone know? Maybe she ... senses something. And when she dies, and her spirit flies free ... I can't say what her spirit will or won't know.

LUCY: *(Snorts.)* Spirit! When did you get so metaphysical? If she ever had a spirit, it flew the coop long ago. Did you ever look into her eyes? Bottomless pits. Totally empty. Except for one thing. That crazy don't-get-in-my-way-or-try-to-stop-me look when she needs some more potato juice. Don't ever get between her and her potatoes! She'll run you over! No, don't worry. I'll never blame myself.

ADELE: How do you know? You're a kid. Eighteen years old! How do you know how you'll feel when you're thirty or fifty or seventy? Wake up, Lucy! This is real. It's not a TV show or a book or some vocabulary game. It doesn't matter how rotten she was or how you feel about her. She's your mother, period. She's dying. Don't you get it? You have one mother. She dies once. I don't want you to wake up some day and realize you blew it. You could feel guilty about that for a long time.

LUCY: She's the one who should feel guilty! Come on, Adele. Don't you remember anything? How about our dog? Have you forgotten how she ran over Tizzy on her way to the liquor store? Bad dog! You got in the lady's way!

ADELE: That was a freak accident.

LUCY: What about my china horses? Crash against the wall! Have you forgotten the screaming? The fights over nothing? I'm glad she's in a coma. We finally get some peace and quiet around here. No, I won't feel guilty, Adele. I'll be glad I wasn't a hypocrite who pretended to feel something when I didn't feel anything.

ADELE: You feel something, all right.

LUCY: Yeah, annoyed that you're hounding me.

ADELE: Listen to yourself! You're mad as a hornet because Mom wasn't what you wanted her to be and now she's leaving. For good. I understand. I'm mad, too. Forty-three years old! Who dies of alcoholism at forty-three? What a waste! *(She thinks.)* Those Alateen meetings — didn't they warn you about anger? How anger can come back to bite you? "Resentment can be fatal." Didn't they tell you that?

LUCY: About a million times. So what? I hope it is fatal.

ADELE: See? That's exactly why we need to say good-bye to her. So we can start to heal. Please come with me, Lucy.

LUCY: How many times do I have to say it, Adele? I'm not going. *(ADELE looks at LUCY, sets the stuffed animal on the bed, rises, walks toward the bedroom door, then turns.)*

ADELE: There's one more thing you might consider.

LUCY: What?

ADELE: Has it occurred to you that I might want you there? That I might need you?

LUCY: *(Actually, that hasn't occurred to LUCY.)* What?

ADELE: If you won't go for Mom's sake, and you won't go for your own, how about going for me? I need you with me, Lucy. Really.

LUCY: *(Lets it sink in.)* I'm sorry, Adele. I wish I could go. But I can't. Physically can't. My brain won't let my legs walk into that room.

ADELE: Will your heart let your legs walk in there?

LUCY: I don't think I have a heart anymore.

ADELE: Don't give me that, Lucy. *(She starts to exit, then turns again.)* You know, her life wasn't completely wasted.

LUCY: It wasn't?

ADELE: She had us. And we have each other. I love you, Lucy.

LUCY: I love you, too, Adele. *(ADELE exits. LUCY pulls out her notebook and pen.)* Where was I? *(Reading.)* "It always has been the "I" for you, hasn't it, Mim? It's all about the "I" and the ego, which is a hallmark of the alcoholic, so that's no surprise. What is surprising — " *(She considers.)* What is surprising? What was I going to say next? How strange! I forgot what I was going to say. *(She chews the end of her pen for a moment, then throws the notebook and the pen onto the floor. She jumps up off the bed, grabs her shoes and — while tugging her shoes onto her feet — half runs, half hops to the door, and calls out down the hall.)* Wait! Wait for me, Adele! I'm coming with you!

Safe

by Deborah Finkelstein

In this brief but intimate duo scene, two sisters, close in age but distant in time and space, stand back-to-back as mirror images and reflect on a disarming story that offers a harsh glimpse of "unspoken" acts of childhood abuse as they try to come to terms with the haunting specters of their past. Ruthlessly forthright at times, the tormented sisters try to find a clearing in the woods, a safe haven to make peace with a past where the pain began, or be burdened until the end of their lives with the terrible, numbing anguish of what they endured as children.

What emerges is a tender and yet moving confession that unfolds in flashbacks to illustrate the price one family pays when it sinks to the depths of depravity. Although the story may have a sadly familiar ring in today's world, it is still profoundly disquieting to learn what it means to sacrifice one's own self in order to protect someone else's safety and the untold cost of making that choice when innocent childhood dreams are shattered by vicious but inescapable reality.

(The two women start the play back to back, in profile, sitting on the edge of the stage. As the play progresses they rise, mirroring each other, but never touching. A small table sits in the middle of the stage, further back from the edge. A box sits on the table. The audience cannot see inside the box. Inside the box are two receivers from telephones.)

CLARE: After school —

AMY: Late at night —

BOTH: He would come into my room.

CLARE: I fought him.

AMY: I said I'd tell.

CLARE: But he told me,

BOTH: Shut up! Or your sister is next.

CLARE: I thought I was protecting my sister —

AMY: So I kept quiet.

CLARE: I didn't tell my mom —

AMY: Or anyone else.

CLARE: I couldn't do this to Amy. I could handle it, as long as she was safe.

AMY: I couldn't imagine Clare going through it. I wanted to keep her safe.

BOTH: I was trying to protect my sister.

AMY: Clare had bronchitis once, real bad. She missed three weeks of school. So she was sent home, and he left me alone. I wanted her to stay sick. I hoped she'd be sick forever.

CLARE: He left me alone when I had bronchitis, almost a month. Said he felt sorry for me, but I think he just didn't want to catch it. The doctor said not to drink orange juice because it would make the penicillin not work. I drank orange juice every chance I got.

AMY: I thought about drinking Drano.

CLARE: But I couldn't do that to my sister.

AMY: Or my mother.

CLARE: I thought it would never end.

AMY: And then one day Mrs. Stilfen had a heart attack.

CLARE: My field hockey coach collapsed. She rode away in an ambulance. Watching someone I cared about suffer — It was the most shocking, and disturbing thing I'd ever seen. Until they sent us home.

AMY: I heard the door, and thought it was my mother. I thought, finally, an end to this.

CLARE: I'd never been home that early. I opened Amy's door, and there he was —

BOTH: You promised me you wouldn't do this to her.

CLARE: I was still carrying my stuff from practice —

AMY: Clare's field hockey stick —

CLARE: *(Re-enacts hitting him with a field hockey stick.)* You told me you wouldn't do this to her! Never again!

AMY: Blood and brains covered everything. My wall, my bed, my face.

BOTH: I was finally free. *(They face each other near the table. As they each take out a receiver from the box, CLARE speaks softly.)*

CLARE: And that's why I'm in here. *(They each hold the receiver to their ears — this is their only way to communicate now that CLARE is in prison. While holding the receivers, they each touch the imaginary glass in front of them.)*

CHAPTER 3
SONGS OF REGRET AND ROMANCE

"The best and most beautiful things in the world cannot
be seen or touched ... but they are felt in the heart."
— Helen Keller, *The Story of My Life*

Songs of regret and romance foreshadow the failed hopes and dreams of characters coming of age or trying desperately to unravel the threads of the past in order to understand the present. There is a wide array of characters here that will not settle for less than a grand romance or who slide into despair, hopelessness, and just plain irrationality as they struggle with haunting specters from the past. There is a good mixture of character portraits that frame saucy spoofs, tragic tableaux, and scathing satires. The incidents punctuate an inexorable series of events in the lives of characters that spin out of control and inevitably extract their own comic or dramatic retribution.

The monologue and duo scene characters address universal questions about the nature of romance, heartache, and the lack of purpose in a world devoid of any apparent meaning. The lesson learned, of course, is that nothing changes in our lives until we find something — or someone — to truly believe in and pursue with passion. The songs are marked by a compassion and understanding that peers into the half-lit world of the characters to remind us to love, laugh, and find a measure of joy in the brief time we are allotted on this earth.

There is an acute atmosphere of anxiety that hovers over a number of the characters as they try to realize personal dreams or resolve interpersonal conflicts. Against this cold and calculating backdrop, characters are forced to confront the prejudices and self-doubts that have misshaped their view of the world. The insights gained, however, provide a meaningful glimpse of an uncommon, and perhaps unexpected, discovery: We are as much a victim of our own human nature as we are of the cruel misfortune that has been ours to endure.

There is also razor-sharp humor to soften some surprising displays of anger and aggression as characters come full circle and realize that the world is no more than a universal stage and its actors simply comic or tragic players in life's drama. As each song unfolds, a heartwarming lesson is learned and the characters realize that an essential goodness lurks somewhere, even in the worst of us. The characters also learn much about the differences that separate people and the similarities which, in time, might just make it possible to bridge the gap that separates them.

These incisive, finely-etched portraits are sometimes profound in revealing the deceit that masquerades beneath a dazzling veneer of characters whose dark secrets are not only real but also dangerous. We are sometimes left with a lingering doubt that perhaps we have not, for the moment, heard all there is to tell about a character, that sparks of envy, scorn, or resentment may still ignite in a blistering climax of violence. But the songs always seem to strike the right note with a comforting refrain that if the spirit is resilient, renewal and recovery are sure to come in time.

Role Playing

The performance challenge in playing these roles is capturing the comic or somber spirit of lighthearted, genuinely human characters and their valiant struggle to confront awakening or repressed desires. There is very little to be gained in an audition if your performance does not reflect those moments of genuine humor, nonsense frivolity, or the grim and sober reality of the characters. Remember that the characters also exhibit courage and conviction even while engaged in innocent blunders, errors in judgment, or exhibiting basic urges such as anxiety, anger, or fear.

Drawing upon personal observations may help to clarify attitudes, postures, or voices for each character's self-image as it is reflected in the text. Relying on casual observation or planned study of everyday situations may also provide invaluable character insights and has the additional benefit of being more contemporary. Such alertness to interesting or intriguing real-life role models in all walks of life may just provide the germ of inspiration that gives your character portrait striking individuality and distinction in an audition.

Although a number of the monologues and duo scenes exhibit a bittersweet quality in tone, what the characters inevitably discover about themselves and their relationship with others is both positive and purposeful in achieving a greater capacity to understand the pain and pleasure of living life to its fullest. Make sure that your portraits subtly reveal believable vocal or physical changes that appear to take place in the characters and make informed, daring choices in performance that build moment-to-moment anticipation and suspense that is resolved with a climactic resolution.

As part of the rehearsal period it will be important to focus on the language and the tempo of action that underscores a character's attitude or mood. Don't forget, however, to look beyond spoken words in order to identify character actions and reactions in the given circumstances described in the text. Assume a positive rehearsal attitude and concentrate on each *present* moment described in the text to capture an incisive character portrait that is rich in nuance and subtext.

Equivocation
by Bill Cain

This fanciful serio-comic character sketch offers an imaginary glimpse into the life of William Shakespeare's teenage daughter Judith, who is desperate to win her father's attention at any price. Although her father lavishes loving attention on fictional heroines filled with clever wit and raw emotion, he barely notices his own flesh-and-blood daughter. Judith is understandably furious in her own masterful display of wit and word play — as refreshingly original and theatrically bold in her passionate point of view as her famous father.

JUDITH: I don't like theatre ... And I don't like soliloquies. *(JUDITH crosses out a soliloquy.)* So it's odd that I'm the one who has them.

(To audience with disgust) Soliloquies. People you've never met telling you things you'd rather not know ... Because nobody ever tells anybody anything *good* in a soliloquy do they? It's always somebody who just killed his father telling you he's on his way to sleep with his mother. If anybody did that in real life ...

(Rewriting) But people do it in plays as if it was the most natural ... Because — in plays — everybody's got a secret story.

(Nonsense) And he always gives them to the wrong people. As if you needed to know one more thing about Hamlet ... He should give them to a minor character — people's daughters, for instance.

(Then) But that wouldn't work, would it? According to him, a daughter's job is to love and be silent. So — there'd be nothing to say ... Besides, who would listen?

Gee's Bend
by Elyzabeth Gregory Wilder

Set in the historic community of Gee's Bend, Alabama, this eloquent monologue captures the vibrant celebration of the pursuit of equality and justice depicted in the infamous "Bloody Sunday" march across the Edmund Pettis Bridge in Selma, Alabama, on March 7, 1965. Sadie, a mature African-American woman who takes spiritual comfort in the face of inevitable pain and suffering, returns home after defying her husband, Macon, in joining the freedom march only to discover that he has locked her out of their home. Her impassioned response should touch every American regardless of race, color, or belief.

SADIE: Macon? Macon, where you at? Open the door. *(She pounds on the door.)* My eyes. I can't hardly see. They put gas in our eyes. It burns real bad like. I need you to help me. It was real bad there. Bad like you never seen. They beat us, Macon. They was waiting, and when we come up over that bridge they took after us. I put my eyes straight in front of me. Walk strong, I be thinking. Walk strong. I so busy looking ahead, I don't see what come up from behind. Sky goes black and me, I'm on the ground. Taste the blood. But I know the hurt mean I'm still alive. They beat on us, then left us for dead. Folks in they stores all up along the way, they just stand there and watch. We cry out, but don't nobody do nothing to help. Please, Macon. I know you say don't go. But I had to. That man he be beating on me, and I say, Sadie, you stand up. I ask the Lord to give me strength. That man might beat me down, but the Lord he raise me up.

Broken

by Barbara Lhota

Bess, a resourceful and strong-willed young woman with a surprisingly lyrical depth of spirit, suffered a serious head injury as a child and is now trying to persuade her mother, Myra, that she is capable of taking care of an infant baby. Although there are some disquieting moments when we learn that the infant is actually Bess's child, the poignant portrait is a more complicated commentary on our attitudes toward the pain Bess must be feeling as she faces an agonizing decision about the future welfare of her child. There is a profoundly moving pathos in the mother and daughter relationship that surfaces as Bess wrestles with her despair and struggles to decide what better life her child might have if adopted ... while at the same time also striving to find a more meaningful purpose in her own life.

BESS: He just kissed me and he touched me and — and, and they're so little. I can do it. I won't hit my stomach again, Mom. I promise. I promise. And I can work really hard. I wash the tables every day at Hope Center. *(Sits, stares out the window.)* I wanted to have a baby like you. *(Myra smiles.)* Maybe it would look like Dad too. I wanted to do something all by myself. I wanted to show you how good I was. Other people do things all their selves every day. I just wanted to do one thing in my whole life to show you. The lawyer at the church said things just happen sometimes. He also said I could give it up for adoption, but I told him I didn't want to do that. And he said, "Sometimes life isn't always like you want it to be." I don't know. Seems like life is never what you want it to be. I wanted this baby real bad, Mom. I thought I could make you proud. And what if I did want to give it to someone? Like a gift. Someone who knows how to take care of hamsters and stuff. Could I do that? You think we could think about it? *(Myra looks at BESS.)* It's a baby, Mom. It's a little flower. *(Beat.)* At least then, Mom, I would have done something real good in my life? Right? *(Myra doesn't answer. She simply holds her daughter. Lights down.)*

Empty
by Julie Halston and Donna Daley

This extraordinarily clever satire on a marriage that has obviously reached the breaking point features an unnamed woman who returns home and is shocked to discover a most unusual burglary. There is a dark mystery here and plenty of dirty work clouding this hilarious caper. The stunned woman phones her husband in a panic and struggles to convince him that the household has been stripped bare and — the most disturbing criminal act — even their dog Caesar is missing! Although there may be amusing laughter on the surface, there is also a profound sense of betrayal beneath that is abruptly resolved with the husband's unexpected revelation that leaves his wife speechless.

WOMAN: *(On phone)* Oh, sweetheart, you aren't going to believe it. Don't get upset. Someone broke into our house and took everything. Everything! The policeman thinks it was sometime between … Yes, I have the police here now. They're filing a report. Everything is gone. Every valuable we have. Stolen. I just got home twenty minutes ago. The door was locked, so I didn't suspect anything. And … I don't know how to tell you this. The dog. The dog is gone. Caesar must have fled when he saw the burglars. He's the worst watchdog ever. I'm sure he'll come home. I know how much you love that dog. Everything is gone — the TV, the computer, the furniture. The furniture! It looks like no one lives here. They're only material things, though. At least we still have each other.

The police actually had the gall to ask if we had been fighting lately. Imagine! What does that have to do with it? I don't know where we are going to sleep tonight. We can't sleep here. There's no bed, no sheets, no pillows, no towels, not even dirty towels. Who would want our dirty towels? We can't eat. We have no dishes, no utensils. The wine rack's gone — along with all the wine. They took our food, too. They even took the dog's food. Isn't this supposed to be a good neighborhood? How did they leave with all that stuff? We don't even know how they got in! There doesn't seem to be any forced entry. You have to see it.

Can you come home now? I can't hear you. You sound muffled. Honey, what was that? Does someone have a dog at the office? For a second I thought I heard Caesar. There it is again. What? No, I haven't seen a note. What note?

Waiting for Oprah
by Mary Miller

Mia, the youngest member of the 1st Tuesday Book Club, is a precocious young girl with purple hair and a free spirit that masks an incredible insight and understanding of the world greater than her years. In the simplest of language, Mia conveys her turbulent childhood in an emotionally absorbing recollection of her mother's death. Seemingly insignificant strands of thought come together in this original monologue to fashion the eloquent portrait of a young girl on a personal journey of self-discovery from darkness to light. Here, she shares that story with the other women — her surrogate mothers — in the group to explain why Oprah Winfrey has chosen to visit their book club.

MIA: When my mama died they found me in the closet, sitting there like a child waiting for her return, breathing in the smell of her perfume. A mixture of cigarette smoke and vodka! But as long as I was there she felt alive. I should've saved some of her clothes … instead of bundling them up in garbage bags sending them off to the Goodwill as if she'd died twice. *(Explaining)*

She was an alcoholic. It took her three years to finally kill herself. My daddy raised me. He's had custody of me since I was eight. I lived with him for thirteen years. I bought that little house over on Morningside Drive with the money I inherited from Mama when she died. It's not much but I think she would have liked it. You know, she got sober once for almost a year when I was fourteen … but she couldn't take it one day at a time. She kept looking at the big picture. Sometimes the big picture is too much to look at and still hold on. Finally she died of cirrhosis of the liver due to complication with alcohol. Three years ago today. And I wrote and told Oprah. It was one of those mother-daughter type relationship shows. I think Oprah worries sometimes because she doesn't have any children. So I wrote her about Mama and told her about the book club. How we've been together for years and how sometimes your real mother isn't always your birth mother. I never expected to hear from her. I just think Oprah wants to see firsthand. I probably should have told you all about Mama, but it's not the kind of thing you begin a conversation with, *"Hi, my mother died a miserable alcoholic. How are you?"*

I suppose sometimes it's just easier telling Oprah.

Blue Window
by Craig Lucas

Libby, a sophisticated but unpredictable woman, has surrounded herself with an odd assortment of guests at a Manhattan, New York, dinner party. The idle chatter of lonely lives and frustrated dreams is more pathetic than amusing, but a series of ingenious twists brings an uneventful evening social hour to a surprising climax. Libby, still struggling to overcome a gruesome accident caused by a careless workman's oversight, lapses into a chilling narrative that reveals the secret she has been hiding ever since that tragic event. Her sense of loss and search for personal freedom is just one of the random pieces of life's puzzle that forces us to somehow acknowledge that people are really unknowable ... and the nightmarish journey out of darkness inevitably ends in the light of truth.

LIBBY: I was looking out. It was late — late afternoon. Everything was blue — as blue as it can be before it gets black. And Marty said, "Come out on the terrace." I said, "I don't have any clothes on." And he brought me this little robe. And we walked out on the terrace. *(Boo puts her hand over her eyes as if she has a headache.)*

We'd only lived there two months. And he kissed me and I put my head back to look up at the sky. Our reflections were in the glass. And I put my head back; we lived on the seventh floor, there was another above us. *(Griever puts his head back as if sighing.)*

And we leaned — he leaned — I set my back against the rail and it … just … We were gone; we were over. I saw us leave the windows. I looked — past him, my hands reached past him to try to hold something, there wasn't anything … just blue. And I didn't black out. I thought — very clearly … This is bad. This is real. And it's true, you see everything pass before your eyes. Everything. Slowly, like a dream, and Marty was … Marty climbing up me and screaming and we turned … over … once … and … we went through an awning … Sloan's … Which saved my life. And I broke every bone in my face. I have a completely new face. My teeth were all shattered; these are all caps. I was in traction for ten months. And Tom came to see me every week. Every day sometimes. Marty's family. Who sued the building. I mean, they never even attached it to the wall. It wasn't even attached. It was just a rail — a loose rail. There was another one on another floor, the same thing could have happened … I landed on him. I killed him. I can't — *(Norbert moves toward her; she flinches.)*

It's seven years. I'm thirty-three years old. I can't have anybody hold me. I can never be held.

Tomorrow's Wish
by Wade Bradford

Juniper, a shy and reclusive young girl with mild learning disabilities, lives with her grandmother in a small, remote rural town, safely sheltered away from the unfathomable mysteries of the real world. She is impetuous, seemingly innocent, and charming in her fiercely unflinching independence, but also capable of outrageous behavior in a sometimes comic attempt to come to grips with the adult world, or to carve a pathway in her own isolated world. In this episode, Juniper is talking to her older cousin, Megan, as she recalls in detail the bittersweet but bumbling experience of her first — and only — kiss.

JUNIPER: I kissed a boy once. At least I tried. I don't know if it counts if they don't kiss back. But I tried to kiss a boy and it almost worked. Most of the time Grandma and I don't get to see folks much, but we go into town. Sometimes. And Grandma says I just have to be careful to mind my manners, and Grandma says I'm real good at being careful, but sometimes I get so bored in that little town. Only one video store. Only two churches. And the park only has two swings and a pool that never gets filled up anymore.

But in our little town there is a boy named Samuel. He's a bag boy at the grocery store. He does it just right and never squishes the eggs. And he has red hair and green eyes. And ... *(Laughs at the memory.)* Freckles all over his face! And Samuel is so nice. So nice to me and Gram. He would always smile and always say, "Thank you" and, "You're welcome." If he says, "Have a nice day," then you do. That's how good he is at his job. And I always wanted ... I always wanted to be close to him, or to talk to him, without Gram around. And one day when Grandma had a really bad cold I got to go to the store all by myself. And I bought some oyster crackers and some medicine.

Then I got to watch Samuel all by myself. Watch him do his bag boy job. I just stared and stared, trying to count all of those handsome freckles. Then, he asked if there was anything else I wanted. I just whispered, "Yes." *(Pauses, closes eyes in remembrance.)* And then I grabbed him by the ears and Mmmm! *(Pretends she's grabbing and kissing him.)* That was my first kiss. It was the most romantic moment of my life. Until the manager pulled me off of him.

Baby's Blues
by Tammy Ryan

Susan, a troubled first-time mother grappling with intense emotions and strained to the breaking point, slowly comes to terms with the present and, ultimately, with the past as she gives her infant daughter a bath. She is an intriguing and somewhat unpredictable woman weaving in and out of childhood memories of her younger self at age nine and then plunging deeply into an obviously unsettled state of mind. Is Susan's mysterious unraveling of past secrets an imaginary flashback, or is it a macabre incident that we might have preferred to leave unexamined?

SUSAN: I had this weird dream. I dreamt I was taking clothes out of the washer, and there was something dark and sopping wet at the bottom of the washer, jeans or something, and I had to yank to get them out, and when I did, it was the baby. Actually two babies and I had to decide which one was the real baby. They looked exactly the same, but I knew I had to choose one so I did, and dropped one in the garbage can, which landed with a thud and didn't move, so I figured I had chosen the right one. But the baby I kept lay on the changing table with her eyes closed not moving, so I worried I picked the wrong one. The changing table changed into a large piece of white paper. There was a knife lying on the paper. I knew I had to cut her open and find her tiny organs, to discover how they worked. I had to dissect her in order to know if it was the right baby, so I could take care of her. She was splayed on the paper like a little frog and I watched my arm reach for the knife, saw my hand pick it up and push the knife in, like a surgeon. I heard a little pop and then it slid right in, but I couldn't find any organs, just blood, blood in the bathtub, and I couldn't find the baby because she was under the water. All I could see were my own hands holding her under the water. *(Brief pause)* It would be so easy to push her head under the water.

The Adventure
by Eric Lane

In this original monologue, a mysterious, solitary young woman slowly enters the playing space and cautiously moves center stage. There is a quiet, ominous mood in the air that is clouded in mystery. The enigmatic woman resolves the initial suspense as she begins to recall the frustration and lack of purpose in her battle to reaffirm the right simply to be herself. There is an almost mystical quality in her story that raises questions of what we owe ourselves, what we owe others, and what borders between them when we want something better for ourselves, but have no clear idea of how to attain it. So, in the end, the woman comes full circle with appearance and reality still undefined ... and we are left with a growing suspicion that all the world may be little more than an illusion of self-fulfillment that remains forever beyond our reach.

WOMAN: I live over by the railroad tracks. Every few minutes another train passes on its way out of or into the city. There's a lot of noise — sometimes there's so much noise I don't know what Barry's saying. He thinks it's funny and laughs. Sometimes he pretends to be talking, and he doesn't make a sound — so like I'll think something's wrong with my hearing from all those trains.

At night, I like to sit in the living room with the light off. We're so close you can see the train, all lit up. Maybe a man's sitting alone or a woman with her girlfriend coming home from a movie or something. I like to watch them move their mouths and fill in the conversation. Barry tells me to come on to bed, but sometimes I like to sit there and see myself sitting in the front car. Barry and the apartment, they just get smaller and smaller while we pull off.

I know exactly what stop to get off at. I walk out to the beach and get in the water. The tide's strong but gentle and it pulls me along. I get out and lie on the sand. I sleep under the moon, then get back in. The water's stronger now and it pulls me under. I don't think of Barry. I don't think nothing except how cold it feels under this deep. I let it pull me 'til there's nothing left.

I get out of the water, trade my red dress for a blue. I get on the next train and head into the city. Nobody knows me there. No Barry. No one. I pass him on the street and he doesn't even see me. Just some girl in a blue dress wanting to know which way to turn down another block or at the corner. And no one knows me. Not Barry. No one but me.

Miss Witherspoon
by Christopher Durang

Veronica Witherspoon, an eccentric woman scarred by too many failed dreams and relationships, finds the world a frightening place and is particularly terrified when Skylab, the American space station, comes crashing down to earth. Enraged and obsessed by this disaster, Veronica commits suicide and now finds herself in Bardo — the "netherworld" in Tibetan Buddhism — rather than in the idyllic "heaven" she had anticipated. Although the mysterious forces in Bardo keep trying to help her reincarnate, Veronica keeps resisting a return visit to earth because the post-9/11 world is even scarier now than when she was alive. Here is a comically chilling prophecy on current — and perhaps future — events for all who claim to be alarmed about the earth of the future.

VERONICA: Well, I'm dead. I committed suicide in the 1990s because of Skylab. Well, not entirely, but that's as sensible an explanation as anything. Most of you don't remember what Skylab was ... I seem to have had a disproportionate reaction to it, most people seemed to have sluffed it off.

Skylab was this American space station, it was thousands of tons of heavy metal, and it got put into orbit over the earth sometime in the seventies.

Eventually the people on board abandoned it, and it was just floating up there; and you'd think the people who put it up there would have had a plan for how to get it back to earth again, but they didn't. Or the plan failed, or something; and in 1979 they announced that Skylab would eventually be falling from the sky in a little bit — this massive thing the size of a city block might come crashing down on your head as you stood in line at Bloomingdale's or sat by your suburban pool, or as you were crossing the George Washington Bridge, etcetera., etcetera.

And the experts didn't think it through, I guess. Sure, let's put massive tonnage up in the sky, I'm sure it won't fall down. Sure, let's build nuclear power plants, I'm sure we'll figure out what to do with radioactive waste eventually.

Well, you can start to see I have the kind of personality that might kill myself. I mean throw in unhappy relationships and a kind of dark, depressive tinge to my psychology, and something like Skylab just sends me over the edge.

"I can't live in a world where there is Skylab!"

I sort of screamed this out in the airport as I was in some endless line waiting to go away to somewhere or other.

So I died sometime in the nineties. Obviously it was a delayed reaction to Skylab.

So I killed myself. Anger turned inward they say. But at least I got to miss 9/11.

If I couldn't stand Skylab, I definitely couldn't stand the sight of people jumping out of windows. And then letters with anthrax postmarked from Trenton. And in some quarters people danced in the streets in celebration. "Oh lots of people killed, yippee, yippee, yippee." God, I hate human beings. I'm glad I killed myself.

You know, in the afterlife I'm considered to have a bad attitude.

The Baptist Gourmet
by Jill Morley

Although this original stand-alone monologue is not part of a longer script, it is a saucy spoof that is rich in slapstick and satire. The incomparable Tulula, a larger-than-life eccentric southern belle and a galloping gourmet in the kitchen, brings all her charm, and some chaos, to bear on a weekly cable cooking show. She religiously dispenses tasty culinary secrets and juicy tidbits of gossip and rumor like salt and pepper to whet the insatiable appetite of small town wives who routinely tune in to relieve their own boredom, or to catch the latest bulletin on recent scandals. On this week's show, Tulula shares a seductive sweet and sour recipe, with suitable embellishments and a full measuring cup of laughter, that is by her own account "divinely inspired" and seasoned with good spirits.

TULULA: G'morin'! Welcome to Channel Sixty-Four's "Cookin' with Tulula." I'm Tulula Lee May, your Baptist Gourmet and before I lead you in a recipe, I'm gonna lead you in a prayer.

Lordy, Lordy, let me learn. Not to let my soufflé burn. And if it does, oh promise me this. Someone in my kitchen will like it crisp! Amen.

Last night, I was divinely inspired when the Lord came to me in a dream and He said, "Tulula, you are my culinary link to humanity. I bestow upon you the celestial preparation for fried grits."

Ingredients are hominy, cheese, and the life-giving energy to all the Lord's creatures ... fat.

First you baptize your ingredients. (*Throws water on the ingredients with fervor.*) You're baptized! You're baptized! You're baptized!

Next, we finely chop the hominy and the cheese, which I have already done because they won't let me have the air time I need. *(Smiles and winks at a producer off-stage.)* Isn't that right, Jimmy? *(Under her breath.)* Producer Shmoducer.

Then, we take the hominy, the cheese, we put it in a skillet, and *fry it up! Just fry it up! In the name of the Lord! Just fry it up! (Lightheaded, she sits down and fans herself.)* Oh, this is gonna be a good one.

Now, while we're waitin' for the culinary miracle, like waitin' for the second coming, I'd like to read some of my viewer mail. Preacher Mapplethorpe writes, "Dear Tulula, thank you for bringing that fried Caesar's salad to the church bazaar last week. Everyone raved over those cute little baby Jesus croutons. And that parmesan cheese looked like snow in the manger!" Amen.

Tessie Jo Miller from Duncan Road asks, "Dear Tulula, what is the rule of thumb in Southern Baptist food preparation?" Tessie, has your cheese dun slid off your cracker? Just slap on some cheese and *fry it up! In the name of the Lord, just fry it up! (Collapses and fans herself again.)* Lord save us all!

Letter from Madge Peeker on Winston Lane, "How do I make my home fried taters taste like yours?" Madge, I seen the way you fry those taters at the church socials. You just chop'em all up like they was the devil's spawn! With each slice, you must instill goodness and ethics and morality. Handle your taters the way God handles His children and your creation will be as perfect as His. On that note, let's resurrect those grits … *(She tastes them.)* Mmmm, mmmm, just like the Lord woulda made them.

Now, tell your Catholic friends to tune in next week because I'm making fried St. Joan Kabobs! Bye, y'all!

The Soy Answer
by Carolyn West

This dark satire is a zany spoof of zombies with a slashing, biting edge that sheds new light on the darker side of a ghoulish afterlife. Amber Johanson, a perky and resourceful entrepreneur, is pitching vegan health food to a skeptical audience of the grateful undead. As a sales representative for Soy Answers, Inc., the savvy and relentless Amber encourages the assorted zombies to keep in step with the times, and is quick to point out the nutritional value of her company's newest health food, Tofu Brains, as she offers tasty test samples to the kindred spirits. Her tone is deliciously sinister, but there is also a comic recognition of the obvious limitations we may all recognize: It's just not that easy being a healthy zombie these days!

AMBER: How many zombies are here tonight? That's a good number. I know how your day goes. You get up in the evening and right away you're starving. You're craving human brains. Now it's a fact that zombies need the nutrition from a fresh brain. You can't have the canned or pickled kind. So the first thing you do when you get up is track down breakfast. My goodness, you're exhausted. You've just dug yourself out of your grave. You don't have the energy to go hunting. I have the solution. Tofu Brains. It has all the nutrition you need and tofu stays fresh without preservatives for an amazingly long time. Tofu also has astonishing health benefits. Recent studies show that women who eat tofu three times a day are at a much lower risk for ovarian cancer. That's something to think about. And before you raise your hands, I know you're already thinking about the taste. Rest assured, the flavor is just wonderful. It even has the texture of gray matter. We've done taste tests all over the country. We gave people Tofu Brains and the real thing and they could not tell the difference. In fact, in just a moment I'm going to give you the same taste test. I have human brains and I have Tofu Brains and I'm not going to tell you which is which.

My Parents
by Joe McCabe

Here is a colorful and upbeat original monologue that vividly sketches a teenage daughter's impressionistic portrait of her parents. She relies on a cascade of classic clichés and word play to poke fun at parents as they are sometimes seen through the eyes of embarrassed children. The wry and witty perceptions are neither syrupy sweet nor bitterly sour, although at times they may be brutally candid. This spicy, delectable fable captures the fantasy of the adult world as a teenager sees it: half romantic, half hard-boiled, and points out that "children learn from their parents," which means from the good examples as well as from the gross!

DAUGHTER: When Mom first met him, Dad was a diamond in the rough with a gift of gab, a man of the world and a man of his word, and a barrel of laughs who never missed a trick. His big heart was in the right place, and he had an open mind on most subjects. Mom had a mind of her own and a memory like an elephant. She wasn't born yesterday, and she had a good head on her shoulders, but she was a backseat driver who made mountains out of molehills. She looked every gift horse in the mouth. Dad always had the courage of his convictions, but sometimes he seemed scared to death of her, even though her bark was worse than her bite. Money burned a hole in his pocket, but year in, year out, Mom saved all she could for the rainy days to come.

Sometimes he'd put all his eggs in one basket or count his chickens before they hatched, and when he had egg on his face she expected him to eat crow. She'd cry over spilled milk, and she'd beat a dead horse till she was blue in the face. He'd bite his tongue and swallow his pride. He'd bend over backwards for her, but he rarely let her get him down. He'd go the extra mile and look for the silver lining along the way. She never quite put him in his place. Mom tried to put the best face on things, and Dad usually played along with her.

"We Could Make Believe," from *Showboat*, was Their Song. They knew how to make virtue of necessity; they stuck together through thick and thin; they made the best of their hard bargain. Dad was generous. Mom was fair. If it weren't for them, I wouldn't be the way I am. Between them they taught me to keep a straight face and a civil tongue, to keep my eyes open and my nose clean, to keep my shirt on and my fingers crossed. They told me to give life my best shot, to roll with the punches, to live and learn. Mom wanted to have the last word. Dad preferred to have the last laugh.

Doubt

by John Patrick Shanley

This suspenseful and provocative mystery play by Pulitzer Prize playwright John Patrick Shanley is a gripping parable that raises nuanced questions of ethical and moral certainty. When suspicions of improper behavior with a student surface, a dark shadow is cast over a young priest and a game of truth or consequences quickly consumes the characters. In this brief scene, Sister James, a young and somewhat naïve nun, and Sister Aloysius, the crusty and rigid school principal, are discussing Father Flynn, who Sister Aloysius suspects has been abusing a male student. The conversation offers a complex but thought-provoking glimpse at why religion, faith, and the human heart can't always be reconciled when confronted with the crippling power of unreasonable and unbending principles.

(Father Flynn has just left the principal's office after offering his candid explanation of allegations made against him. SISTER JAMES and SISTER ALOYSIUS now share their impressions.)

SISTER JAMES: Well. What a relief! He cleared it all up.

SISTER ALOYSIUS: You believe him?

SISTER JAMES: Of course.

SISTER ALOYSIUS: Isn't it more that it's easier to believe him?

SISTER JAMES: But we can corroborate his story with Mr. McGinn!

SISTER ALOYSIUS: Yes. These types of people are clever. They're not so easily undone.

SISTER JAMES: Well, I'm convinced!

SISTER ALOYSIUS: You're not. You just want things to be resolved so you can have simplicity back.

SISTER JAMES: I want no further part of this.

SISTER ALOYSIUS: I'll bring him down. With or without your help.

SISTER JAMES: How can you be so sure he's lying?

SISTER ALOYSIUS: Experience.

SISTER JAMES: You just don't like him! You don't like it that he uses a ballpoint pen. You don't like it that he takes three lumps of sugar in his tea. You don't like it that he likes "Frosty the Snowman." And you're letting that convince you of something

75

terrible, just terrible! Well, I like "Frosty the Snowman"! And it would be nice if this school weren't run like a prison! And I think it's a good thing that I love to teach History and that I might inspire my students to love it, too! And if you judge that to mean I'm not fit to be a teacher, then so be it!

SISTER ALOYSIUS: Sit down. *(SISTER JAMES sits.)* In ancient Sparta, important matters were decided by who shouted loudest. Fortunately, we are not in ancient Sparta. Now. Do you honestly find the students in this school to be treated like inmates in a prison?

SISTER JAMES: *(Relenting.)* No, I don't. Actually, by and large, they seem to be fairly happy. But they're all uniformly terrified of you!

SISTER ALOYSIUS: Yes. That's how it works.

Freedom High
by Adam Kraar

Henry, a mature African-American young man determined to fight injustice and discrimination, has been training white student volunteers to travel to the South as part of the Mississippi Summer Project and help with voter registration campaigns during the 1960's Civil Rights Movement. Although he wrestles with doubts about the project, Henry is committed to speak out in the face of the unspeakable cruelty and exploitation he sees eroding the heart and soul of his people.

In this duo scene he is confronted by Jessica, a young white college student from an upper class background, who is alarmed about the increased tensions that are erupting between Henry and some of the other student volunteers. The surface bickering has left Jessica crushed and disillusioned. She decides to confront Henry about the increasing despair and skepticism that is eroding the student volunteers' spirit of commitment as they train in the woods near a college campus in Ohio.

(HENRY enters, walking quickly, carrying a small branch he's torn off of a tree. JESSICA comes up behind him, out of breath.)

JESSICA: Henry … wait.

HENRY: You followin' me?

JESSICA: I just wanna ask —

HENRY: You don't wanna talk to me right now. Dig?

JESSICA: We weren't laughing at you. We're laughing at the documentary. That pink lady, rambling on about how Negroes don't want to vote?

HENRY: Go talk to Roz.

JESSICA: *(Blocking his way)* You're the one keeps saying we're gonna get killed. Is that what you really think?

HENRY: Yeah.

JESSICA: So — what? — we should disband the whole Project?

HENRY: Just … leave me be.

JESSICA: Henry, the whole future of the Movement —

HENRY: You're not part of the Movement, okay?

JESSICA: Oh, yeah?

HENRY: Yeah. You're just a …

JESSICA: What? Rich white kid?

HENRY: I got nothin' against you bein' white, but once you're in Mississippi, it's … it's not a game —

JESSICA: I know.

HENRY: You don't! You don't know. And that's why this Project is … 'Cause not only you gonna get killed, you gonna get all of us killed.

JESSICA: So why, why did you come here? *(HENRY waves this off and starts to walk away.)* You at least owe me —

HENRY: I don't owe you nothin'.

JESSICA: *(A new tack)* No one was paying attention. Now they are.

HENRY: Summer's gonna end. All'a you gonna go back north. And so are the cameras.

JESSICA: I won't leave at the end of the summer. I'll stay —

HENRY: You won't last a month.

JESSICA: You don't know me. I may be a klutz, I may say too much, but there's more to me … You're being just as bigoted … as they are.

HENRY: Who?

JESSICA: Those people in Mississippi —

HENRY: *(Appalled)* What?

JESSICA: It's the same thing. You create all these tests — Of course we're not gonna live up to what you can do. That doesn't mean we're incapable — I know, I know I haven't seen the kind of violence you have. But when I heard about those girls, torn to pieces in their Sunday school? I cried; I had nightmares —

HENRY: Not the same as a bomb going off in your kitchen.

JESSICA: I'm sure you need to tell us about that. But I know — I know! — what it's like to be invisible. I'm invisible to my own family!

HENRY: I hear you, but —

JESSICA: I also have great capabilities — great, vast capabilities! — that I have not been given the chance to ... You think just 'cause I went to Radcliffe, I haven't known discrimination?

HENRY: You better off joining the Peace Corps —

JESSICA: No! If we don't go to Mississippi, what's going to happen? Where's it gonna end? Talk to me!

HENRY: I don't know where it's gonna end.

JESSICA: More killing? A race war? That what you want?

HENRY: It's not about what I want, what you want. Jesus! The dogs are outta the pound. They smell blood. *(He stops himself.)*

JESSICA: What are you talking about? You got something to say? Say it! I don't know the way it is? Tell me.

HENRY: Things I been seein' 'round the country.

JESSICA: *(Curious, receptive)* Yeah? Like what?

HENRY: Like, I was up in New York City, spent time with some Negro teenagers. They livin' in buildings a lot more disgusting than a Mississippi sharecropper. They go a mile downtown and see white folks with money fallin' outta their coats, and then go uptown and the police tells 'em they can't play on the street. Man, when it gets hot up there, and they get chased off the streets ... somethin's gonna blow.

JESSICA: Is that why you changed? *(We hear a dog barking, getting closer.)*

HENRY: We gotta run — Come on!

JESSICA: Hey — Look, it's just someone's pet. See? *(Man's voice calling off-stage to a dog, "Come on, boy." The barking stops. Pause.)* We're not in Mississippi yet ... Hey, you know, I have a car here. What do you say we get off this campus, go into town, and get some lemonade? I bet you haven't even been in town yet. Come on, we won't even talk about the Project.

HENRY: Promise?

JESSICA: Cross my heart ... Come on. *(They exit.)*

Mr. Lucky's
by Stephen Fife

When Alison, a spicy single young woman with a hard-boiled exterior, inadvertently meets Tom, a breezy single young man with a roving eye, at the fairly upscale Mr. Lucky's Bar, comic sparks begin to fly in this saucy duo scene of the battle of the sexes. After one fleeting glance, each is singularly impressed with the other and they go head-to-head in an attempt to define what it is that young men and women want these days when searching for a "dream" partner.

What begins as another slice-of-single-life comedy about a chance encounter and the search for true love and meaning, quickly escalates into a witty duel of wits between two loners on the prowl for acceptance and happiness ... but burdened with their own assorted personal demons. Their exchanges are delicious barbs delivered with subtle asides to the audience that resemble a contemporary comedy of manners — until a fatal blow is delivered by Alison and the comic interlude draws to an abrupt end on a rather wet note!

(TOM and ALISON are seated on bar stools.)

TOM: *(To audience)* I've been sitting here a few moments, just taking in all the ambience: the burnished wood and low lighting, the posters of showgirls from the Ziegfield Follies — girls who are dead now, it's true, but my ... what legs. I look around, and I have a really good feeling about this place. A better feeling than I've had about any place in a while ... I'm pretty sure I've never been here.

ALISON: *(To audience)* I come to this bar all the time. All the time. No one interesting ever comes here.

TOM: I passed by this place lots of times, I'm sure of that much. Lots of times before tonight. I really don't know why I never came in.

ALISON: It's like there's a sign on the door. "Interesting guys stay away. Pathetic morons are welcome."

TOM: Maybe it was the name. Yeah, I guess that was it. "Mr. Lucky's."

ALISON: Once or twice I saw someone. Some guy. He'd sit down and nod at the bartender, then order a draft in a confident voice. My interest was piqued, I glanced over, flashed him my best cryptic smile `...` Then he'd look back, he'd turn the full force of his gaze on me, and I'd see the words printed right there on his forehead: "More of the Same."

TOM: I was a little put off at first, ya know, that's a lot of pressure to put on a guy. But now I think I can deal with it. I think I've gone through enough bad times that I'm ready for something good. Yeah. "Mr. Lucky's."

ALISON: "Mr. Lucky's." Yeah, right. I guess that's why I came here in the first place. Walked in off the dark street one night, the street filled with muggers and stalkers and shaking little jars filled with their vital fluids, and plopped my rear down on this overstuffed barstool. Just to prove a point, to prove that name was all crap. *(Pause)* I think I've more than succeeded. *(She drains her drink, stands. ALISON and TOM glance at each other. Their eyes meet. Pause. Both look away. ALISON sits.)* Wow.

TOM: Wow.

ALISON: Wow.

TOM: Wow.

ALISON: What planet did he beam down from?

TOM: Wow.

ALISON: I'm afraid to look over again, I'm afraid he's gonna be like one of those premium channels you're not supposed to be getting ...

TOM: Wow. I mean — wow. She is exactly ...

ALISON: I'm afraid he's gonna suddenly fade out or else his face will be all scrambled up, with black lines across it ...

TOM: I mean, exactly. Exactly.

ALISON: You're crazy, Alison, really crazy. Your reception doesn't pick up this station. This isn't part of your package.

TOM: It's like she walked right out of my brain and sat down on that barstool and ordered a drink. It's like a chunk of my brain is enjoying a drink there. *(Pause. TOM glances over at ALISON. She glances at him. They can't avoid catching each other's eye.)*

TOM: Hi.

ALISON: Hi.

TOM: How's it goin'?

ALISON: Good.

TOM: Good.

ALISON: How's it goin' with you?

TOM: Good.

ALISON: Good. *(Pause)*

TOM: Good. *(Pause. He looks away. To the audience)* Oh god.

ALISON: *(To audience)* God.

TOM: Good. Good. What is that?

ALISON: Good, Alison. Good. That was real good.

TOM: Beer nuts are good. Cheeseburgers are good. Joe Crocker Live at the Hollywood Bowl is good. But this is not good.

ALISON: See, this is the thing. I've talked with so many morons, I can't even remember what real people say anymore. People who actually eat with a knife and fork.

TOM: *(To ALISON)* Can I get you another drink?

ALISON: What?

TOM: Can I buy you another drink?

ALISON: No.

TOM: Okay.

ALISON: No, I'm just fine.

TOM: Okay.

ALISON: Thank you but no. *(Pause)* No, thank you. *(Pause)*

TOM: Me too.

ALISON: What?

TOM: I'm fine too. With my drink I mean.

ALISON: Oh.

TOM: Yeah ...

ALISON: Oh.

TOM: Yeah.

ALISON: Good.

TOM: Good.

ALISON: Good. *(Desperate pause)*

TOM: *(To audience)* Ah.

ALISON: *(To audience)* Ooooh.

TOM: *(To audience)* Come on, think of something ...

ALISON: *(To audience)* This is like a nightmare ...

TOM: *(To audience)* I can't be this stupid ...

ALISON: *(To audience)* I can't be this stupid ... *(Pause)*

TOM: I didn't mean to insult you.

ALISON: What?

TOM: I mean, I hope I didn't insult you. Before. When I asked …

ALISON: Who says I felt insulted?

TOM: Well, the tone of your voice … I thought maybe —

ALISON: Believe me, I don't feel insulted.

TOM: Well, good. I'm glad. It's just the way you said no. There was just so much … no in it.

ALISON: Oh, you would know if I felt insulted, believe me.

TOM: Yeah?

ALISON: Yeah. There would be absolutely no question about it.

TOM: Huh. Well, I guess I was wrong then.

ALISON: I guess you were.

TOM: So you have a real temper, huh? I think that's good. I mean, healthy. You live longer that way.

ALISON: See, this is what I would've done if I felt insulted. *(She tosses the contents of her drink in his face. The liquid drips from his face.)*

CHAPTER 4
SONGS OF ILLUSION AND REALITY

"The soul should always stand ajar ...
ready to welcome the ecstatic experience."
— Emily Dickinson, *Poems*

Songs of illusion and reality dare to introduce fanciful theatrical parables, enriched with probing character portraits, to expose the disquieting secret that dreams and reality are often one and the same, with the ultimate "truth" somehow out of reach. Often humorous and frequently quite sober, the characters will keep you amused, guessing, and puzzled as they stumble from one paradox of human nature to another. We also catch a fleeting glimpse of the aberrant personalities, frustrated passions, and preposterous prophecies that run the gamut from idealistic to idiotic.

The characters blend comedy, irony, and satire — sometimes dripping with tragic pathos — to illustrate the vast chasms and intimate crannies that define complex human relationships. Comedy is found in the most unlikely places, irony in the funniest pratfalls, and satire in the most tragic circumstances — all to help us define the illusion and reality of our own lives. We must also come to terms with our share of communal folly and guilt for not allowing dreamers like these to make their fantasies come true through a realization of themselves, rather than what we had hoped they would become.

The dreamers here do try, on occasion, to make their illusions come true by probing into the damaging truths secretly hidden in the lives of their friends. They also piece together illusory tales of fabricated transgressions, festering guilt, alienation, and betrayal or tortured, long endured insults and injuries never forgiven — nor forgotten. Some will create their own magical world to conceal shattered hopes and dreams, or spend their lives lamenting the abandonment and indifference of family or friends. Still others will transform themselves into mock human beings surrounded by an entourage of adoring groupies, would-be fellow traveling companions, or casual acquaintances in order to recapture cherished hopes and dreams of the past.

The realists, however, insist that the only thing that seems to stand in the way of their success is a failure to conform to far-fetched tales of wise wizards and wistful kingdoms, foolish notions of true love forever after, or fantasies where the villain is punished and virtue rewarded. They are prepared not merely to justify but also to defend the ends through which their means are attained: It is the wiser course to accept for the best what cannot be changed for the better.

"Realists" do not sing about cherished dreams of the future. Quite the contrary, they struggle to build predictable lives and find stable relationships in a real world constantly under siege from unpredictable tectonic shifts in their lives that twist or turn and then culminate in an explosive, surprise ending. For realists, all ends as it should end with evildoers punished, true lovers united, and an inevitable return to a more comfortable pattern of life, which time and old age can only deepen. Weary of the world's vain flattery and cynical duplicity, realists have taken a solemn oath to speak only the truth, no matter what offense this might give to others who view life through rose-colored glasses or through a funhouse mirror.

Role Playing

Playing these roles requires ingenious or "offbeat" approaches to highlight character intention or motivation. The first step, of course, is to determine if your monologue or duo scene character is a dreamer lost and lonely in a subjective world of make-believe, or a realist that strikes a note of directness and simplicity in an objective world of day-to-day reason. When that choice has been made, your primary performance objective should be to appear believable and sensible no matter what the situation or the character behavior indicated in the text.

It is best to "generalize" these characters with careful attention to vocal quality, facial expressions, and subtle gestures that mirror the interior feelings or thoughts suggested in the text. Do not allow yourself to distort or exaggerate the meaning of the words spoken or the actions taken by your character. Allow the incongruity between what the dialogue says and what the character does in subsequent action to suggest the laughable, the ludicrous, or the lamentable.

Concentrate on the basic humanity that accompanies the dreamer or the realist in their search for a meaningful identity. It may be useful to chart bodily actions and gestures to communicate significant character emotions or thoughts. You may also wish to integrate appropriate personal traits or mannerisms to reinforce the character portrait. If you can clearly identify and then "visualize" the world of the character, your audition performance will suggest a more three-dimensional interpretation that has meaningful subtext.

Another principle at work in these monologues and duo scenes is the need to be truthful to the character's nature and to pay careful attention to the personal opinions expressed by the character in order to determine if they are believable. Being able to clearly distinguish reality or illusion in a character's dialogue and subsequent action will help you more clearly understand the final choices at play in a character's internal or external struggle. Being able to discover the answers to these questions will also give your monologue audition heightened dimension and distinction.

The Weir
by Conor McPherson

Valerie, a mysterious young woman from Dublin, has recently moved to a distant, rural part of Ireland. Here she sits quietly in the local pub listening intently as the locals swap bizarre ghost stories. One of the lurid yarns concerning a small child obviously disturbs her, and she quickly retreats to the ladies' room. When she later returns, an increasingly agitated Valerie insists that she would like to share a story about her five-year-old daughter, who died the previous year in a swimming pool accident. What follows is a haunting tale of a grieving mother who seems to be pleading with us for forgiveness and understanding.

VALERIE: I was in bed, Daniel had gone to work. I usually lay there for a few hours, trying to stay asleep, really. I suppose. And the phone rang. And I just let it. I wasn't going to get it. And it rang for a long time. Eventually it stopped and I was dropping off again. But then it started ringing again, for a long time. So I thought it must have been Daniel trying to get me. Someone who knew I was there.

So I went down and answered it. The line was very faint. It was like a crossed line. There were voices, but I couldn't hear what they were saying. And then I heard Niamh. She said, "Mammy?" And I … just said, you know, "Yes."*(Short pause)* And she said … She wanted me to come and collect her. I mean, I wasn't sure whether this was a dream or her leaving us had been a dream. I just said, "Where are you?"

And she said she thought she was at Nana's. In the bedroom. But Nana wasn't there. And she was scared. There were children knocking in the walls and the man was standing across the road, and he was looking up and he was going to cross the road. And would I come and get her?

And I said I would, of course I would. And I dropped the phone and I ran out to the car in just a tee-shirt I slept in. And I drove to Daniel's mother's house. And I could hardly see. I was crying so much. I mean. I knew she wasn't going to be there. I knew she was gone. But to think wherever she was … that … And there was nothing I could do about it.

Daniel's mother got a doctor and I … slept for a day or two. But it was … Daniel felt that I needed to face up to Niamh being gone. But I just thought that he should face up to what happened to me. He was insisting that I get some treatment, and then … everything would be okay. But you know, what can help that, if she's out there? She still … she still needs me. *(Pause)*

Glass Eels
by Nell Leyshon

Lily, a confused and emotionally fragile young girl, struggles to confront her own internal conflicts with faith, spirituality, and the intrinsic value of human life. The only person she is able to share her nightmare story with is Kenneth, a family friend who has known her all her life. Here, late at night, Lily is mysteriously drawn to the river where her mother died and where thousands of eels are stirring as they anticipate their solitary migration to the sea. Lily now recalls a childhood memory about her father and appears to be asking us what went wrong … and why.

LILY: I think I'm like my mother.

She came down here at night.

I know I shouldn't come, but I can't stop myself.

I know she came here. Sat here. Swam in there.

She's not in the house anymore.

I used to look for her. I found things she touched. I found a piece of paper with her handwriting. I found a shoe in the garden. A dress she'd worn.

It hadn't been washed.

(LILY sits up.)

I want to tell you this thing. But I don't want you to look at me. Look away. That's it.

If you look at me I'll stop.

I used to think everyone had dead bodies in their houses. I'd go in the room where he got them ready. He caught me one day, looking at the powder he used on their skin to tighten it. I was gonna use it on me but he took it from me, said it was only for dead skin.

I started going down at night and if we had one I'd lift the sheet from their faces.

I used to think if I looked at them long enough I could bring them back to life, make them breathe again.

One night there was a new one there. I took the sheet and peeled it down. Stood and stared.

It was my mother.

(Kenneth looks.)

No. Don't look at me.

It had happened late at night and no one had woken me to tell me. That's how I found out.

Her skin was streaked with mud. Her hair still damp from the river. A piece of weed in it.

(Pause)

I stood there and tried to make her breathe again. Tried to make her chest move.

Nothing happened.

So I reached out and pulled her eyelids up, to get her to open her eyes and look at me. But her eyes had rolled back and there was just the whites.

I tried to pull the lids back down but they had stuck.

I had to go upstairs and into my dad's room. I had to tell him to come with me, to see what I'd done.

He followed me down and I showed him.

He saw and then he turned and grabbed my arm, too tight. He shook me and screamed at me, told me I shouldn't have gone and then he hit me. Here. *(Touches face.)*

Some things that happen to you, you get them in here.

(Touching face) And you can't get them out.

I wish you could take it out so I didn't have to remember it.

Tales from the Arabian Mice
by Will Averill

In this gender-neutral excerpt, Rock, a perennial bit player with a somewhat naïve sense of the art of theatre, sits waiting for that "big break," which is sure to come despite all the obvious obstacles and frustrations that surely lie ahead. Chock-full of self-confidence without ever having played more than a walk-on role in the theatre, Rock offers a telling commentary on one rather disturbing illusion about the acting profession: The cherished belief that inexperienced newcomers seeking to make their way in theatre can achieve quick success, instant happiness, and a meteoric rise to stardom if they simply believe in and pursue their dream, without also experiencing frequent episodes of rejection and heartache.

ROCK: Hi. I don't know if you remember me or not, but I was the kid who played the Crocodile last year in *Peter Pan?* Do you remember? Probably not. It was a little part, and although I've trained for years for a life in the theatre, three years running here at the [insert name of venue], they have neglected to use me to my fullest potential … again. You know what I am this year? I'm. a. rock. Not the professional wrestler and famous actor in such cinematic classics as the *Scorpion King*. No, I'm just a routine lousy geological formation which our protagonist (that's a big word for hero that I learned in my three years of professional theatre training, all of which did me *no* good when it came to casting), finds himself [herself] collapsing against in his [her] time of trouble. Can't wait for school to start again — "We went to Disneyworld this summer, oh, wow, we went to Europe. Hey, what did you do this summer [insert name]. Who, me? Oh. I stayed at home *and played a lousy 'rock'!* Not that I'm bitter. 'Cause it's — *(Uber-sarcastic)* — it's great training."

Oh. Excuse me. Gotta go *lie on the floor and do nothing* now for a while. *(ROCK returns to his [her] position.)*

Phantom Rep
by Ben Alexander

In this original character sketch, Christie, an impressionable and troubled young actress searching for acceptance in life, has been inadvertently locked in the theatre with Monica, a rival actress who accuses Christie of using the potential fame and glamour of acting simply to feed her own vanity. In a vigorous defense of these accusations, and in an attempt to reconcile the tangled strands of her own life, Christie reveals a transformative incident in her youth that reveals she is not nearly as vain or villainous as she might appear to be at first glance.

CHRISTIE: It was in the third grade, when they took us for a field trip to see *Richard III* in Boston. I'd never seen a live play before. I didn't understand what was going on up there, but I could tell that there was a whole bunch of people hating each other, going to war against each other, and just plain killing each other — kind of like all the wars and murders I heard about on the news. The last hour, I was really spacing out, desperately bored and upset with it all, wanting to go back to class and just take a spelling test or draw a picture. Then finally it ended and they closed the curtain.

But then — right then — they did something that I wasn't ready for. They opened the curtain again, and there was everybody who'd been running around hating each other and killing each other for the last three and a half hours — they were all up there, holding hands, smiling at each other, patting each other on the back, smiling at us, taking a nice bow, and that was when it really hit me. Hit me hard. They looked so beautiful, so peaceful and loving. Richard the Third was standing right next to the woman he'd murdered, and she was holding his hand and smiling at him as if they were about to go get something to eat together as soon as they washed off their makeup and changed their clothes. And I had that picture in my head all the way back in the bus, and I lay awake in bed practically all that night, thinking, that's what the world needs.

We need to get the U.N. to pass a resolution that on a certain Sunday, everybody in the world — the President of the United States, the head of Russia, the murderers, the bank robbers, the millionaires, the coal miners — will just line up and hold hands and take a bow. Dead people, too. I decided that dead people would suddenly be able to get up off the floor, walk over to the guy who killed them, and say, "Good show, good show. Ladies and gentlemen, we were only kidding. It was all a story. We really all love each other, and now we're going to change out of our costumes and have a party. You can all come too. Cake and cookies and wine, all on us!" And that's why I wanted to act: So I could do that. Whether I was playing Snow White or the stepmother, Cordelia or Lady Macbeth, I wanted people to see me get up off the floor and take my place in line, smiling and holding hands with everybody, so I could give them a taste of what it would be like if the whole world could take a curtain call.

The Baltimore Waltz
by Paula Vogel

This fantasy by Pulitzer Prize playwright Paula Vogel is based on the wily adventures of a darkly comic brother and sister, Anna and Carl, one of whom has been diagnosed with a fatal disease. It is Anna, the unmarried schoolteacher, who has been diagnosed — mistakenly we later discover — with ATD, an Acquired Toilet Disease with an extremely high risk factor for elementary school teachers! The medical nightmare that follows sends a hyperventilating Anna and a captive Carl spinning off to Europe to find a cure, and perhaps some romance among the ruins, before life's final curtain call. On the first night in her hotel room, Anna has a difficult time sleeping and suddenly springs upright from a harrowing dream.

ANNA: I feel so alone. The ceiling is pressing down on me. I can't believe I am dying. Only at night. Only at night. In the morning, when I open my eyes, I feel absolutely well — without a body. And then the thought comes crashing in my mind. This is the last spring I may see. This is the last summer. It can't be. There must be a mistake. They mixed the specimens up in the hospital. Some poor person is walking around, dying, with the false confidence of my prognosis, thinking themselves well. It's a clerical error.

How could this happen to me! I did my lesson plans faithfully for the past ten years! I've taught in classrooms without walls — kept up on new audio-visual aids — I read *Summerhill!* And I believed it! When the principal assigned me the job of the talent show — and nobody wants to do the talent show — I pleaded for cafeteria duty, bus duty — but no, I got stuck with the talent show. And those kids put on the best darn show that school has ever seen! Which one of them did this to me? Emily Baker? For slugging Johnnie MacIntosh? Johnnie MacIntosh? Because I sent him home for exposing himself to Susy Higgins? Susy Higgins? Because I called her out on her nose-picking? Or those Nader twins? I've spent the best years of my life giving to those kids — it's not — ...

Sheets of Rain
by Lexanne Leonard

In this original monologue, Terri, a gritty and street-wise young woman who works as a waitress at a typical small town diner, remains hopelessly trapped in her mother's haunting, idealistic dreams of Hollywood stardom. In this stammering strain of pent-up memories, she painfully paints a blistering portrait of her loneliness ... of the grim struggle to wrestle with the negative forces of life and her fate. This simple tale of a young woman's coming of age raises larger questions about the boundaries of love and the need to look to the future despite all present odds. Terri's story is an honest and unsparing glimpse of a mother and daughter relationship shattered by the destructive forces of self-sacrifice and self-destruction that cannot be tempered or toned down.

TERRI: Hi, Joe. I'll set you up. *(TERRI gets Joe coffee and a doughnut.)* They say it's going to rain again today. Can you believe that? We're in the middle of the desert and we get rain. *(She pours a large glass of water for Joe.)* Again. How much rain does that make so far this year? Seven inches? My room smells moldy, like my grandma's living room. *(Touches her reflection in the glass.)* Did you know my full name is Therese Marie Hart after my grandma? Terri's my nickname.

My mom wanted to name me Rita after her favorite actress. Grandma said no. Mom was a rebel but wouldn't rebel using her new baby girl as ammunition. So she played the good mom role as long as she could. She yearned to give me a chance to have the best of everything. She thought that going to Hollywood would be the answer. She said I would be a star. She wanted me to have a big house with a swimming pool. She dreamed of cocktail parties. Women with red lips and tiny waists in bathing suits and high heels. Men with dark curly hair in long white terrycloth robes drinkin' it straight up.

So, when I was six, she piled the two of us into the '55 Nomad in her black and white striped bathing suit with the big brimmed hat and crimson high heels. I was excited. She refused to look back. She worked a lot of jobs. Egg candling. Cleaning sparkplugs. Inspecting meat. She was good at that one. That's why we never ate pork. She wanted me to become the best. Classes. Dance. Etiquette. Modeling. I was always going somewhere.

At night she would read to me from *Alice's Adventure in Wonderland.* When we finished she would take me over to a mirror. *(Holds a large spatula in front of her face like a mirror.)* She would kneel down and touch her head to mine. With both of us looking in the mirror she would say, "Look. Go ahead. You'll be surprised. What do you see?" No matter how hard I tried, all I saw was me and her and bits and pieces of wherever we were. But when I looked at her face in the mirror, I could tell that she was seeing something different. She was always making me look into mirrors. Sometimes when she powdered her nose, she would push her compact in front of my face and say, "Can you see it?"

Eventually the jobs dried up along with her dreams. There was no more money for my classes that promised to make me famous. So she was forced to look back. On our way back to Grandma's we stopped here. Suzie liked my mom and gave her a job without her even asking. Mom liked the girls. They talked and joked while they worked, flirting with the customers. Suzie let me do my homework sitting on this stool where I wasn't in the way, but where she said I could watch everything. Suzie said it was important to watch everything. How else would you know about life? I learned how to do algebra while watching everything. Watching the girls flirt was the most useful though. (She tries to flirt with an imaginary customer sitting at the counter and then grabs the coffee pot to pour Joe more coffee. On her way, TERRI stops at the window — her gazing spot — touches the glass and rubs it with the edge of her hand.)

Did you ever wonder how Alice got through the looking glass? Was it like she was a ghost and floated to the other side? Or maybe it magically parted inviting her to step through. Or did she have to break it? *(Raises the coffee pot in her hand and starts to throw it through the window. Joe moves to her, takes the pot out of her hand, squeezes her shoulders, and guides her back to the counter.)*

It was raining that day, too. They call it sheets of rain. You couldn't even see the street through the window. To me it looked like funhouse mirrors. You could see the shapes but they were distorted. When I came through the door, Suzie met me with a towel. I was dripping. She said Mom had to go somewhere but she would be back shortly. To warm me up, Suzie gave me a cup of coffee with lots of milk and sugar. I don't like the taste of coffee. She told me not to worry and to finish my homework.

She took me to a table near the back. She said she was cleaning the counter. I couldn't watch the door from there but at least I could see its reflection in the window. Good. I could still watch the world. In the reflection, sitting at a table, I noticed a man with black curly hair. As I was getting my books out, the door swung open and my mom hurried in out of breath. The whole diner turned on her smile. She was soaked.

You could see her bra through her white uniform clinging to her body. Her skirt pressed against her hips and legs. She was barefoot.

I started to her for my afternoon hug but the curly haired stranger enveloped her in his arms before I could take a breath. "Come on, Hon. We gotta go." She pushed him aside with a flirty smile and checked her hair in the window. She wasn't pleased. She stepped around the stranger and found me, motioning for me to come to her. "Terri, this is Rick. He works at the studios. He says he can get me a part in a movie he's working on. Suzie said you can stay with her until we get settled. I've packed everything in Rick's car. We'll be back soon. Here's his phone number. I'll call." A quick kiss and hug and they were gone. Through the funhouse mirror into a car I couldn't tell the color of.

Men & Cars
by Diane Spodarek

Maggie, a full-blooded, sassy single mother and musician, has a fascination with and need for ... men and their cars! Perched seductively on a tall stool at The Last Exit Bar, she is brittle, blunt, and wonderfully brass in this original, vintage snapshot that recounts how the legend of men and their cars has been passed down from generation to generation. There is an air of mystery and intrigue that surrounds the self-confident Maggie as she spins her tall tale for the amusement of the patrons. We observe the complex relationship and deep bonds that exist between the caregivers (men) and those receiving care (cars), and discover, much to our amusement, the fine line that separates normalcy from insanity in this fiery vehicle of social satire.

MAGGIE: I like to drink a tall Bud when I'm walking around the streets of Manhattan. I keep it in a brown paper bag and sip it through a straw. Sometimes I like to stand on the corner and wait. Wait for the men. You ever watch men and their cars? Ever watch men look under their cars? I like the way men look when they look under their cars.

I like to watch men sit in their cars, start them up, find out they don't start, get out, look at the car, then go to the hood. Open the hood, look in, go back to the inside of the car, and try to start it up again. Get out again, look under the car, look at the ground, look at the spill on the ground, look all around, sometimes at their companion, if they're with someone. If not, look for another man in the vicinity to share this moment. Then there are two or three sometimes four men looking under the hood or looking under the car, or at the ground.

Sometimes they stare at each other and they get that look. I like that look. It's somehow familiar. I can't put my finger on it, I can't really say what it is, but it just gives me a funny feeling watching them, the men and their cars, although I don't really think it has anything to do with the fact that I'm from Detroit.

Senior Square
by John-Michael Williams

Rochelle, a young, impulsive high school student who lives in her own theatrical world of make-believe, walks on-stage carrying a large purse, combing her hair, and looking intently into a handheld mirror. She has a colorful, fertile imagination and etches some memorable portraits of the trials and tribulations of a high school sophomore on a treacherous journey toward the day she eventually becomes a senior and is suddenly catapulted to "celebrity status." Rochelle, powdered and perfumed with a façade of glamour, now dreams of finding her proper place in life as an actress ... and the prospects for her success will no doubt be questioned long after the stage lights have dimmed!

ROCHELLE: I'm goin' to a Madonna Film Festival at the public library tonight and, well — you never know *who* will be there, so it's always best to be beautiful. *(Sliding on a streak of lipstick.)* Is that too much lipstick? *(Holding a small mirror up to her face and then looking up toward the sky.)*

This light is very bad — but a girl learns to cope. I'm gonna be an actress when I graduate. Then I'm changing my name from Mary Rochelle Ridgeway to Rochelle Ridge, though I hope the producers won't nickname me Rocky. Can you imagine? Rocky Ridge? *(Pause)* Though, on second thought — Rocky's kind of sexy don't you think? They call Raquel Welch "Rocky" and she's sexy, right? Yeah, Rocky

Ridge. Does it sound too tough? *(Pause)* Well that's okay, because an actress has gotta be tough. *(Putting on eye shadow.)*

Eye shadow says it all, doesn't it? All the really famous actresses in America wear it. It's an American tradition — like apple pie, corsages on a date — hot dogs at a ball game — it's practically patriotic — just like Senior Square. *(Pointing)* That's it. Right in front of me. *(Horrified)* No, I can't step in! I'm only a sophomore and — *(Taking a small booklet out of her jacket and flipping it open)* according to Chapter Three, Paragraph Six of the Student Handbook, "Any non-senior apprehended within the boundaries of the Square is in violation of Article Six of the Central High School Constitution regarding the essential traditions of the institution." I know. Heavy *stuff*. And if a senior catches you in there, you — *(Looking into the book again)* "Will be required to scrub the interior of Senior Square with a toothbrush or made to stand on your head during the Friday Pledge of Allegiance in the Auditorium." I would just die. *(Dabbing on powder)*

Seems like a small thing, being able to walk inside a brick enclosure and sit down, but for a lot of kids in my school, Senior Square will never be anything more than another broken dream. Many will not graduate for one reason or another and you can never predict who'll make it and who won't. Bobby Giangelo was voted most likely to be elected Senior King, even though he was only a sophomore and his twelfth grade days were two years ahead of him. Bobby had it all, good looks, good grades, good attitude, good family *(Pause)* good looks. *(Pause)* Oh yeah, money. Bobby loved school and everybody at school loved him, but a lot of money can buy cocaine and Bobby just burned out. Like a bulb that glowed too bright for too long. "Socket warp" we call it. *(Applying rouge)*

Like the color? Oh, thank you. Rouge is very tricky. Too little, you look anemic. Too much, you look like Ronald McDonald. Other kids get bored, or married, or both, then drop out. Some, just kinda fade away. And there are the ones who get so close to Senior Square that they can almost touch it but never make those last few steps. So, in its own way, it's really something special, something everybody wants, though few kids will admit it. And those who say that Senior Square is just a brick fence surrounding a couple of picnic tables — those are the kids who really want it the most. *(Pause)* I plan on having the lead in the school play during my senior year. I truly hope they'll do *Gone with the Wind*. Oh, I know it's a movie but they can change it to a play for me. Scarlett O'Hara is a sweet, frail, innocent young virgin in a desperate search for true love — a *perfect* role for me. *(Pause)* Don't you think so?

A Day of Turning
by Todd Caster

Laura, a hard-driving but caring young paramedic in this original monologue, has just experienced the death of a young boy under her care on a trip to the hospital. In this compelling blend of gut-wrenching honesty she confesses to a coworker the reason why she decided to become a paramedic. Laura's intimate confessional serves to point up a moment of shattering emotional impact — her mother's suicide — and her own dogged resiliency. Now a dazed survivor, Laura relives that searing moment of truth from childhood and is, finally, able to make peace with herself now that the nightmare has become a dream … a dream, however, that still goes on.

LAURA: I had him, Bobby — you were there. You saw I had him. How did it go so wrong? *(Listens to Bobby.)* You can't win 'em all? That's your answer? Maybe that's what I should have told his parents? "Mr. and Mrs. Kowolski, I'm so sorry about your boy. I know you trusted me to keep him alive on that ambulance ride. But if you don't mind me sayin' — you can't win 'em all!" *(LAURA takes a water bottle and drinks.)* It's not you, Bobby. I know you mean well. It's not you. It's me. I'm damaged. Like something broken. And … I'll never be right.

Did I ever tell you why I decided to become a paramedic? It's a great story. A real jewel. I was nine years old the day it happened — the day of turning. *(Pause)* Thanksgiving dinner, there we were. Our "perfect" family — all together. My mother and I had cooked all morning, making most of the meal from scratch. It wasn't much. Not that we ever had much — just a few scraps held together by a fistful of creativity. *(Pause)* My father had been drinking since he rolled out of bed that morning, so by the time dinner came around he was in his rarest form. Let me explain something to you. When Daddy drank, he wasn't one of those sloppy, happy drunks. We weren't that fortunate. No, the more he drank, the meaner he got. And the meaner he got, the more focused he became. He'd find one little thing to pick at and he'd grab on for dear life. Like a junkyard dog with a bone, he wouldn't let go. *(Pause)*

Something my mother did that day — something of no consequence, I am sure — and my father pounced. He cursed her. He berated her. On and on he went, right through the meal. Finally, I'd had enough. I pushed my chair away from the table, stood up, and raised my glass to a toast. *(LAURA raises her water bottle.)* "To a Happy Thanksgiving!" I said as bravely as I could. Then I made a suggestion that we go around the table. Each one of us should name one thing that we were thankful for.

I could see Daddy out of the corner of my eye, not looking too pleased at my suggestion. But in the end he agreed, though not without a smirk. I started out just to break the tension. Then it went around to Maddy and Darryl. When it got to "the drunk," we braced ourselves for his answer. I'll never forget his words. Not in a million years. "What am I thankful for?" He said, "That God invented bourbon whiskey, to wash this pig slop down!"

My mother quietly folded her napkin, brought her plate to the sink, and left the room. I guess that was her answer, about what she was thankful for — absolutely nothing. *(Pause)* Later that afternoon, after us kids had finished cleaning up, with Daddy passed out in his chair, we went looking for our mother. Being the oldest — and, in turn, the bravest — I was elected to knock on her bedroom door. "Come in," she said. Right away I heard a "clunk," like something toppling over — and then a creaking sound. Can you guess how this ends? She'd been standing on a chair, with a lamp cord around her neck, waiting for somebody to come looking for her. Maybe she expected Daddy to be the one to find her. I can't say. The point is that she needed someone to witness this final act. Any one of us, or all of us would do.

At first I didn't understand what was happening. Everything was all mixed-up and backwards. The room was filled with this loud piercing noise. The noise, I soon realized, was a shriek bubbling up from the bottom of my throat. I begged. I pleaded. I tried to lift her up, but I didn't have the strength. I tried to cut the cord, but I couldn't reach it. I sent Darryl to get Daddy, but he was dead drunk and passed out. I was trapped. Helpless. All I could do was look into her accusing eyes and watch the life drain out of her. *(Long pause)* That's when my destiny first spoke to me. I'm never going to feel that helpless ever again.

Cruising Close to Crazy
by Laura Shaine Cunningham

Carolee Crockett, a celebrated, self-conscious, and aging singer with a talent for making choices that end in disaster, takes a look at the bruising world of country western music in this original, slashing documentary on the curse and the salvation of celebrity. She is speaking from the cramped bedroom of her tour bus to confirm the rumor that she refuses to be "honored" at this year's award show along with her ex-lover and singing partner. Carolee's wild ride of passion and heartache offers a backstage glimpse of jealousy and passion that leads us smack dab into the crisis of a tortured country western star who feels life gave her an inch when she deserved a mile!

CAROLEE: *(Speaking nonstop with broken energy)* My mouth's so dry, I can't talk. Nine times in the hospital this year. Nodes. Ain't suppose to sing, that's how come I'm on the road, doing two shows a night, in thirty-six cities. I got letters from doctors all over the world, say, "Carolee, don't sing, don't speak, don't even open your mouth." There's one doctor so big, he's too big for the Mayo Clinic, that's how big he is, took one look down my throat, and said, "Don't even open your mouth for a year, Carolee, don't speak, even to me." *(Pause)*

So I kind of nodded at him, then went right back on the road. I can't do my people that way. God respects you when you work, but He loves you when you sing. *(She roots through the piled bedding, finds a baggie, and pops a pill.)* Where's my nerve pills? I thank God, I'm not on dope. *(She swallows a few more pills.)* This just Percodan, for my back. *(She takes another pill.)* Clears your head real good, too. I just had a sharp thought. *(She blinks.)* It was passing through. *(She shakes her head, woozy.)* Well, it'll come back. Always do. *(She gropes along the vanity shelf and accidentally knocks off a Styrofoam head.)* Didn't like that one much, anyway — I had another kind of nerve pill, it was better than most. It was the only one could stop my bad dreaming.

(She squints at the audience.) You ever dream you were dead? And it was so real, you was surprised to find you wasn't? Only you wake up, it ain't that different? *(She shivers.)* I have been having dreams so bad, I can't sleep. I'm afraid to put down my head, that's the truth. *(She shudders.)* I was wearing my violent dress, I was in a wine-colored coffin, in a wine-colored room. Everybody in the business come pay their respects. They was all around me, whispering, "Oh, ain't it sad, don't she look sweet?" But they was drinking beer and eating chicken legs, too. Earl Wayne. Norbie. The Duker ... Honey Bascomb. They was all there, saying how great I was, but it was a bunch of bull. They were all just thinking — "Now, she's dead, even her old albums will sell." *(Thoughtful)* Well, it worked for Elvis. He gone gold.

(Sighs.) I had to lie there, listening to all their bull, like they wasn't the ones put me right where I was. *(Imitates simper.)* And they were saying, "Oh, don't she look beautiful, ain't she finally at peace." Meanwhile, they got the new album piled up outside the funeral home door. Too bad I can't get out of my coffin and sign them. And you know, the entire time, the entire time, I'm just laying there, waiting for him to come in. *(She squints at the audience.)* And you know which one. There's only one ever really makes you crazy. Oh, there's some can get you going, make you a little nuts, but there's only one, can kill you. And don't you know? He don't even show. He done me dead like he done me alive.

(Angry) And now they want me standing next to him in the auditorium lined up with all a them so we can be the Cavalcade of Fools ... I can just see it. Him and me, crowned fools of country music, salutin' to our own stupidity. Winding up with "Amazin' Grace." *(Croaking lyrics)* "Oh, I'll fly away ... " *(Bitter)* I'll fly away, all right. I've flown. *(Shudders.)* I'm dying. This old bus is going to be my hearse. I'm dying, and there's nobody to care.

The School Mascot
by Amanda Kozik

This original character portrait features the darling Amanda, a naïve but nimble high school freshman who carefully shields herself from the outside world by dressing up as the school mascot ... a giant sewer rat! There is a merry blend of slapstick and offbeat hilarity in Amanda's antics and exploits as she meets each crisis with a healthy dose of venom. She may be a fearless hero figure to other introverted first-year students, but to wise-cracking upperclassmen, Amanda is just one more nerd to keep in line. Here she is reconciled to yet another defeat in her young life and prepared to transfer to a different school next year. Amanda leaves, hopefully, a wiser person whose real values in life might lie elsewhere than in the goals she so furiously pursued as a giant sewer rat.

AMANDA: Most people would think being that goof who dresses up as the school mascot would be fun. Most schools have mascots like Tigers, Vikings, Bears, Knights, or Lions. I wanted to get involved with that thing that they so strangely titled "school spirit." I tried out, since last year's mascot had moved to another school in Vienna. I was a freshman, and like one I was determined to get the part. I tried and the coach was saying, "Are you sure, don't you know ... " I know all the details I told him. I figured it was because I was a girl that he was so hesitant. How was I to know my school's mascot was a giant sewer rat? After all I hadn't been to any pep assemblies yet.

I get beat up on a daily basis. First, because I am the reject mascot, second because I'm also president of the chess club, and third because I'm fifteen and still wear a training bra. If I was head cheerleader I would receive respect from my peers, even though sometimes some of the most peppy cheerleaders have an I.Q. of fifty-seven. My friends were supposed to keep my identity as the despised mascot a secret, but instead they told the whole school.

I guess the reason I haven't quit yet is because of the intimate relationship I hold with the guys' varsity football team. After the homecoming game the fullback and the quarterback both gave me a present, a barrel of blue Gatorade over my head. One time the opposing school tried to kidnap me, while in costume, as a practical joke. The police finally found me, locked in an extra large dog carrier on the side of the highway.

I guess I really should spend more energy on the chess club. I win more matches than the two other members. By day I'm your typical nerd, but by night I'm a giant sewer rat! Next year I'm moving to Vienna for the same reason last year's mascot did, a chance to change my identity. A word of advice to any freshman of next year: School spirit is actually something you'll find in creepy ghost stories. Listen to me, or you may find yourself parading around as a giant sewer rat!

We Cannot Know the Mind of God
by Mikhail Horowitz

This lighthearted, joyfully explosive short play opens with a rueful God visiting Adam and Eve — whose purity of heart and abiding faith appear to be shaken by boredom — in the Garden of Eden. It is a fast-paced, sharply written morality tale with gentle bruising humor and profound humanity in its treatment of redemption and the miracle of rebirth. Familiar biblical characters spring to life with sidesplitting one-liners and offer stinging satirical insight of ethereal, spiritual, and, at times, irrational matters. These are the eternal questions that puzzle us all ... and the ones who do not seek to find an answer are those who have truly lost their sense of humor.

(Note: Brad and Buffy may be played by Adam and Eve.)

GOD: So let me get this straight: you've assigned a name to everything in the garden — appellated all of Creation, as it were — and now you're ... bored?

ADAM: Well, at the risk of sounding ungrateful ...

EVE: ... or of insufficient intelligence to amuse ourselves in any meaningful way ...

ADAM: ... or, for that matter, in any unmeaningful way, since amusement, as we know ...

EVE: ... or *would* know, assuming we'd eaten from the Tree, but, uh, we haven't, so, uh, hey, scratch that ...

ADAM: ... since amusement, as I was saying, need not be instructive or edifying, but may simply be experienced for its own sake ...

EVE: ... but yes, in point of fact, and by no means do we intend this to be disrespectful, or in any way dismissive of your largesse ...

ADAM: ... but yes, now that you mention it, we are utterly, totally, absolutely bored.

GOD: Hmmmm. Well, I did anticipate something of this nature.

EVE: *(Whispering, to ADAM)* Well, like, *duh,* he is omniscient, right?

ADAM: *(Whispering harshly back)* Ssssh! He's also omniaural, okay?

EVE: *(Whispering)* Omni — what?

GOD: All-hearing, but let's pretend I didn't hear that. No, I did anticipate that protracted exposure to paradise would render it pedestrian, eventually ... cause you to become a bit jaded with Creation. But I do have something in mind to make the time pass a little more swiftly, a little more engagingly. I propose we play a little game.

EVE: *(Warily)* And, uh, this game is called ... ?

GOD: The game is called "I'm thinking of something." You see, I'll think of something, and you have to guess what it is.

ADAM: And, uh, the point of this being ...

GOD: *(Sighs.)* The point of this being to provide a small diversion, since you and Eve have deemed such necessary, from the otherwise dreary and deadening perfection of your ideal existence in this flawlessly conceived, impeccably crafted habitat. Shall we begin?

ADAM: Uh, okay.

EVE: Hey, we'll give it a shot.

GOD: Very good. Now then: I'm thinking of something. Can either of you tell me what I'm thinking of?

ADAM: Is it ... something having a nacreous color?

GOD: No.

EVE: Is it ... something stridulating at the edge of a meadow?

GOD: No.

ADAM: Is it ... something concealed in a bearded spruce?

GOD: No.

EVE: Is it ... something phosphorescing on a jetty?

GOD: Uh-uh. *(The Q & A gets faster.)*

ADAM: Something basking on a crag?

103

GOD: No.

EVE: Something squalling in a den?

GOD: No.

ADAM: Something swooping over a lake?

GOD: No.

EVE: Something whimpering in a ditch?

GOD: No.

ADAM: Is it something confectionery washing away in the rain?

GOD: No.

EVE: Something splendidly bound in morocco gilt?

GOD: No.

ADAM: Something woven painstakingly from the fiber of wild Iris leaves?

GOD: No.

EVE: Something with several large transversely striated muscular fasciculi that radiate from the sides of the thoracic ganglion?

GOD: Uhhhh … no. *(The Q & A slows down again.)*

ADAM: Something, uh, something that, uh, something about a million degrees Kelvin at its core?

GOD: No.

EVE: Something, uh, something poops round pellets that look like black tapioca?

GOD: Nice image, but no.

ADAM: *(Weakly)* Something that … something that … say, why has my hair fallen out? And most of my teeth?

EVE: *(Drooping.)* I can't seem to keep my eyes open. And when did my back start hurting like this?

ADAM: Ack! I can barely raise my head. How long have we been playing this game?

GOD: Well, by your time, you've been playing this game for, oh, sixty years, eleven months, and seven days, and now you are both dying. I told you it would divert you!

ADAM: *(Very weakly)* But … but we still haven't guessed …

EVE: Is it … something disturbingly out of place in a bowl of wonton soup?

GOD: Nnnnn-nupe.

ADAM: Something … that naps … in the shade of a … baobab …

(ADAM and EVE slump motionless to the ground. Enter ANGEL of Death.)

ANGEL: Sir?

GOD: Yes, Death?

ANGEL: We have innumerable descendants of Adam and Eve, sir, all waiting to play the game.

GOD: Very well. I suppose we've got to accommodate them all, to keep them from screaming bloody murder at contemplation of your blameless odiousness. Well, send them in, send them in. Who are these two?

ANGEL: Brad and Buffy Abramowitz, sir, from Bergen County, New Jersey. *(ADAM and EVE awaken, rubbing their eyes.)*

GOD: Thank you, Death. And shut the black hole on your way out.

ANGEL: Very good, sir. *(Exit ANGEL of Death)*

GOD: Brad, Buffy, I'm thinking of something. Can either of you tell me what I'm thinking of? *(ADAM and EVE are now BRAD and BUFFY.)*

BRAD: Is it … something that makes a crunchy, tart addition to a simple lettuce salad?

GOD: No.

BUFFY: Is it … something of faded radiance catching the eye from the bottom of a junk pile?

GOD: No, Buffy, but I like the cut of your jib.

BRAD: Is it … something rancid in an artist's refrigerator?

GOD: Sorry.

BUFFY: Is it … something described by an art critic as "a caravan of erratics deposited by a minimalist moraine?'

GOD: God no, but that's a good one! The lights begin to fade.

BRAD: Wait, wait! Is it something … uh, is it something with a long, uh, you know, one of those whaddayacallums, you know, one of those?

GOD: Not even close.

(Blackout)

The Gazing Ball
by Dwight Watson

This unique, truly original short play treats time and place with the insight and vision that leads the characters from initial inhibition and suspicion to a heartfelt, rewarding resolution of unrestrained acceptance and joy. On a warm spring afternoon, Lydia, a young woman in her late teens with the carefree innocence of youth, cautiously approaches the front porch of a neatly manicured suburban home carrying a wicker baby basket. With the dappled sunshine shimmering brightly overhead, Lydia quietly, gently places the basket on the porch and starts to scurry away, only to be abruptly halted by the shocking voice of Maggie, the self-assured homeowner, who steps briskly out of the house to snare the intruder.

There, amid the wisteria blossoms and a blue ornamental gazing ball that rests on a pedestal near the porch, the two seemingly different women come together to form a subtle yet eloquent whole, which illuminates the way in which separate lives are really connected in ways not readily apparent even to those involved. The women voice the simplest dialogue to convey a broad and meaningful theme: The journey through life (happily) provides chance encounters needed to achieve personal understanding and acceptance of others powerless to find their way in this world. Their conversation, deeply revealing of lost hopes and dreams, is also a touching account of the sense of humanity we all so desperately seek in life.

MAGGIE: Hey, stop! Come back here. I said stop! *(LYDIA freezes.)* Now, turn around, and come here. *(LYDIA inches her way back to the porch.)* Closer. Closer. Now tell me. What are you doing?

LYDIA: *(Quietly)* Nothing.

MAGGIE: *(Pointing to the basket)* Did you leave this here?

LYDIA: *(Avoiding MAGGIE's stare)* No.

MAGGIE: It's yours, isn't it?

LYDIA: *(Meekly)* I don't know anything about it.

MAGGIE: I saw you through the window. I saw you walking down the street carrying this basket a few minutes ago.

LYDIA: *(Unconvincingly)* I don't know anything about it.

MAGGIE: You left it here, didn't you?

LYDIA: I … ah … don't …

MAGGIE: *(Perplexed)* What were you thinking?

LYDIA: *(Feeling trapped)* I don't know.

MAGGIE: I know it's yours. This basket is yours.

LYDIA: *(Twisted)* I … ah …

MAGGIE: How could you? How could you do that?

LYDIA: What?

MAGGIE: Just leave the baby and walk away. What were you thinking?

LYDIA: *(Quiet confession)* I don't know.

MAGGIE: What if I didn't see it? What if I didn't come home for lunch and see it? What then?

LYDIA: Really … I don't know.

MAGGIE: *(With growing frustration)* What if I had decided to go away for the weekend, had stopped the mail and the newspapers, and no one came out here for days?

LYDIA: *(Apologetically)* I didn't think about that.

MAGGIE: How long would it have survived?

LYDIA: Survived?

MAGGIE: Without attention. Without care. If I had gone away, leaving it here on the porch?

LYDIA: *(Weary)* I'm sorry.

MAGGIE: I know what you were thinking. You were thinking that I have a professional obligation to take care of it, didn't you?

LYDIA: I didn't know you were a nurse.

MAGGIE: I didn't say I was a nurse.

LYDIA: You dress like one.

MAGGIE: What were you thinking?

LYDIA: "Just find a nice warm spot." That's what she said. "And leave him there."

MAGGIE: Who said that?

LYDIA: A woman … at the shelter.

MAGGIE: *(Incredulously)* She told you to leave the baby in the sun?

LYDIA: Yeah.

MAGGIE: What was her name?

LYDIA: *(Truthfully)* I don't know her name.

MAGGIE: What is the name of the shelter? I want a name.

LYDIA: *(Trying to explain)* I don't know the name. But I had to do something. And so I've been walking around all morning looking for the right spot. When I saw your place, I thought, "This is it. This is where he belongs. This is what she meant."

MAGGIE: You thought I would take care of him?

LYDIA: I just know it looked like the right spot.

MAGGIE: The right spot?

LYDIA: *(A confession)* I like the way the sun shines on your porch, the flowers, green grass, and trees. I like the way you feed the birds and give them water to drink and splash. I've walked all morning and I've seen a lot of homes with bird baths, but when I saw this round, gazing ball on the stand, here, next to your door, I was drawn to it … because it was like the glass ball my mother put out front of my house when I was little. She said the ball was called a Globe of Happiness, and that no home should be without one … because, you see, it kept witches from entering the house.

MAGGIE: And how is that?

LYDIA: Because witches think they are the most beautiful creatures in the world. And when they look into a gazing ball, they fall so in love with their own reflection, they cannot pull themselves away. So, I knew this home was protected. And that there are no witches inside. And that's why I left him here … with you. Is that true?

MAGGIE: What?

LYDIA: There are no witches inside?

MAGGIE: No. No witches. *(Moved by her story)* How old is he?

LYDIA: A few days.

MAGGIE: Does he have a name?

LYDIA: I call him … Little One.

MAGGIE: Can I see him?

LYDIA: Yeah. Be careful, he's very small, under the blanket.

MAGGIE: I will.

LYDIA: Because, he's very little.

MAGGIE: *(Unfolding the blanket, taken back, studies the bird, and then LYDIA.)* It's a bird. A baby bird.

LYDIA: Yeah. He fell out of his nest. I found him.

MAGGIE: *(Putting it together)* And you called the shelter. The animal shelter.

LYDIA: They told me to leave him in sunshine.

MAGGIE: I thought you left me a baby.

LYDIA: *(Avoiding MAGGIE's gaze.)* Yeah.

MAGGIE: Your baby.

LYDIA: *(Quietly)* Yeah.

MAGGIE: *(After a moment, a realization)* Do you have a child? An infant?

LYDIA: *(Worried, confused)* Yeah.

MAGGIE: What are you going to do with him?

LYDIA: I don't know.

MAGGIE: *(Sympathetically)* Do you need some help?

LYDIA: Yeah.

MAGGIE: *(Reassuringly)* Yeah. Well. You've come to the right place.

LYDIA: *(Breathing deep)* I thought so.

CHAPTER 5
SONGS OF FAITH AND FOLLY

"I know why the caged bird sings, ah me,
When his wing is bruised and his bosom sore.
When he beats his bars and he would be free;
It is not a carol of joy or glee,
But a prayer that he sends from his heart's deep core."
— Maya Angelou, *I Know Why the Caged Bird Sings*

The beauty and ugliness of hopes and dreams sacrificed to the harsh realities of life have been compressed into these monologues and duo scenes. They offer remarkable glimpses of a character world where faith or folly play a major role in the journey of self-discovery. Resolute faith and a belief in the last-minute intervention of saving grace or an act of kindness sustains a number of the characters towards the inevitable dawning of a bright new day. For the most part, however, more skeptical characters experience a less picaresque adventure and are left stranded, crushed, or disillusioned along the way.

Characters are either forgiving or vengeful in their bickering about stinging injustices, petty prejudices, or failed struggles to overcome mistrust and doubt. Underneath this rippling stream of consciousness runs a very deep reservoir of angry, lonely, and guilt-ridden frustration that foreshadows some cataclysmic eruption just around the corner. Only then, perhaps, will we be able to hear the voices of faith and folly singing happily in the distance and know they have, finally, been able to create a new world out of the chaos of the old.

Written with bold and boisterous strokes that combine ethics and morality with stark realism, the characters here offer no simple answers for the cynical songs they sing off-key. They will all, before the fateful end, take a leap of faith or folly and face their own distorted or twisted truths. The deepened insights that surface underline a more universal truth: We must all seek life's true values patiently and with purpose before we can hope to find answers to the problems that plague mankind.

While exploring their human condition, characters also come to terms with hidden truths that lie beneath the surface of their raucous humor or somber satire. These songs are a testament to the eternal quest for truth, love, and virtue. They weave a compelling tapestry of real-life people and their values as they come to grips with crushing reality. The lessons learned about growing up, going on, and accepting what life or a perverse fate imposes on us is made starkly clear. There must always be hope, however futile, and the ways of the world must be accepted … if not always understood.

Role Play

In playing these roles it is important not to allow the emotional content of the episodes to serve as your primary focus. Try to isolate the "central action" and apparent "conflict" of each character, and then create an *interior monologue* based on the central action and apparent conflict to better understand the motivation and subtext of the character. It may be helpful to paraphrase lines of dialogue to better understand the context of the monologue or duo scene and to incorporate subtle stage business that helps to more clearly define your character portrait.

These monologues, in particular, will need a close reading to provide a working blueprint for an audition. At first, it is well to read each monologue with an active ear for clues to character interpretation and movement hints. A second reading should be more critical and focus on any implied subtext being conveyed in the words or actions of the character. A third and final reading should polish a well-defined interpretation of the character's point of view, detailing the visual and aural approach you will take in an audition.

Playing these roles should encourage you to rely more consciously upon your "memory book" of life experiences, or observed behaviors and mannerisms, to add subtle nuances of interpretation to a dynamic character portrait. A more conscious use of the memory book approach to character definition underscores the basic similarity between a character's thought and action with a real-life model. It should also help you to translate abstract ideas or concepts suggested by the text into audition strategies that engage *both* the voice and body in defining a character's mental or physical activity.

Be mindful, however, to use movement sparingly and concentrate on each character's mood or attitude. Knowing your character's specific goals or objectives and the physical actions that help communicate them will help you perform in a consistent and convincing manner. You should pay particular attention to the emotional or intellectual conflict of characters in their struggle to express anxiety, frustration, or turmoil that has surfaced in personal relationships with other characters in the text. Finally, be aware of the fierce sense of independence and plaintive urgency voiced by the characters as they share private confidences or solemn confessions related to their frustrated aspirations or dreams.

Reckless
by Craig Lucas

This dark, murky comedy is a holiday fable that offers a blunt study of the homeless and vagrant culture of society. Instead of a typical sociological treatise, this study focuses on the deteriorating ethical and spiritual condition of the characters. On Christmas Eve, Rachel, who daydreams of a perfect middle-class life, discovers that her husband has hired a gunman to kill her. She flees to the home of her friend Pootie, a paraplegic who has been pretending to be deaf in order to pursue a relationship with Lloyd, her physical therapist — and to also receive double disability checks. Here, Pootie recounts first meeting Lloyd at a clinic and little by little we witness someone desperately reaching out for love ... Unfortunately, the values Pootie has been pursuing most of her life appear to have been tarnished by deceit and deception.

POOTIE: When I lost the use of my legs a friend drove me up here to Springfield to take a look at this place where they worked with the handicapped. I watched the physical therapists working with the patients and there was one: I remember he was working with a quadriplegic. I thought he was the most beautiful man I'd ever seen. A light shining out through his skin. And I thought if I couldn't be with him I'd die. But I knew I would just be one more crippled dame as far as he was concerned, so my friend helped to get me registered as deaf and disabled. I used to teach sign language to the hearing impaired. I thought if I were somehow needier than the rest I would get special attention. I realized soon enough that everyone gets special attention where Lloyd is concerned.

But by then it was too late. He was in love with me, with my honesty. He learned to sign; he told me how he'd run away from a bad marriage and changed his name so he wouldn't have to pay child support. He got me a job at Hands Across the Sea and I couldn't bring myself to tell him that I had another name and another life, that I'd run away too, because I owed the government so much money and wasn't able to pay after the accident. I believe in honesty. I believe in total honesty. And I need him and he needs me to be the person he thinks I am and I am that person, I really am that person. I'm a crippled deaf girl, short and stout. Here is my wheelchair, here is my mouth.

Organ Failure
by Andrew Biss

The standard romantic tale of "the other woman" demands a more contemporary version and this original, finely-tuned monologue offers a bright new angle with a twist of sardonic irony likely to become a classic. In this retelling of the romantic myth, the other woman's façade of affection and kindliness is stripped away to unceremoniously reveal the brash reality of a bold and cunningly ingenious lover. It is a stark portrait of the anguish and crippling dependency the other woman paints when she addresses her lover's body in the viewing room of a funeral home. Now determined to forge a new identity from the one she has always known, the other woman has apparently broken the bonds of servitude and achieved some degree of independence with surprising results!

THE OTHER WOMAN: Well, well, just take a look at you ... all scrubbed and polished and ready for inspection. I have to hand it to them, they really did a good job on you. Who could imagine you now that such a short time ago you were lying in a pool of your own vomit, your organs finally having decided to give up on you ... just like everyone else.

(Beat)

Except me.

(Beat)

What did they stuff in your cheeks? Cotton, is it? Or some synthetic stuff? No, I think it's cotton ... the look, the feel of cotton. Cotton mouth — how appropriate. Well, whatever it is, it's a good look for you. You were always so gaunt and drawn, but now you look ... well, quite lively. What a shame. Still, it'll make for a good send off. And like they say, you never get a second chance to make a lasting impression.

(Beat)

I will miss you, you know that, don't you? Despite all those years of being second-best to ... well, just about everything really: the wife; later, the ex-wife; the job; probably the dog. And, oh, let's not forget the all-consuming, never-ending, neurotic bouts of introspection. If you'd been any more self-absorbed you'd have turned into a black hole. Just a small one, though. And last but not least, of course ... the bottle. Though under the circumstance, I suppose that goes without saying. Yes, I think it's fair to say the only thing in your entire life you ever committed yourself to fully and unreservedly was the bottle. And look how it's thanked you.

(Beat)

But, like I say, I will miss you. Because as awful as it is ... was ... it was what I knew. I knew it wasn't good, I knew I wanted better, but it was what I had ... and I accepted it as such. There's a dealer in life, you know, and he's throwing the cards across the table, and the person next to you gets an ace and you get tossed a five of diamonds, and you think to yourself, well, that's the breaks. And you don't have to blame yourself for what happens, because you can blame it on the dealer. It's an easy out. And I took it. I went along with it all, and as lousy as it got, I could always console myself with the knowledge that I wasn't to blame. And in my head I guess I made the dealer my enabler. Kind of like you and your liquor store clerk, I'd imagine. So, yes, accepting your dregs became a way of life. And like anything you get used to, once it's gone you miss it. Doesn't mean it was any good ... it was just always there.

(Beat)

But on the occasion of our last conversation ... something changed. Not in you; certainly not in your voice. That was the same, slurred, barely comprehensible, self-pitying rambling I was oh so very used to. No, it was ... in me. Something in me ... somehow ... heard you differently. The feeble, garbled plea for help was just the same. My response — dropping everything and rushing over — was just the same. But inside ... inside of me ... well, I guess one of my organs quit on you, too. I didn't feel a thing.

(Beat.)

You see, what you don't know is ... you were still alive when I got there.

(Beat)

I looked down at you, crumpled in a heap on the floor, battered and bruised from yet another bender session of flailing around blind drunk. You weren't conscious but you were breathing. And I thought to drag you to your bed and get you cleaned up a bit, just as always. But I didn't. I decided to sit in the chair and contemplate things — contemplate you. And the longer I stared at you, the further away you seemed. After a while it was as if I was staring at someone else. Someone I didn't know. And then you began to vomit.

(Beat)

Your body started jerking violently as the vomit forced its way out of your mouth and nose. But you were still unconscious and breathing it back in, your throat choking on the acid, gasping for breath. And I sat in that chair watching you drown ... until finally the struggling stopped and everything was quiet and still. And I waited ... waited until I was sure the peace was permanent ... for both of us.

(Beat)

Then I called for help ... even though neither of us needed it. Because, you see, sometimes in life ... well, you've just got to help yourself.

The Waiting Room
by Lisa Loomer

This astonishingly timely comedy is an unadorned and unrelenting ride through feminist and medical politics. It depicts the disturbing descent into a cold and unforgiving reality some women must confront each day when faced with the possibility of a cancer diagnosis. Wanda, a mature woman who has watched too much Marilyn Monroe — while experimenting with too many cosmetic surgeries and silicone injections in her timeless quest for physical perfection — has just been informed that she has a tumor that may be malignant. In the struggle to come to terms with the possibility that her idyllic world may be torn in two, Wanda leaves the hospital and walks across the street to a bar. There, in quiet solitude, she tries to piece together the puzzle of her life, while recalling a bet she made with her mother five years earlier.

WANDA: I got home last night, I had six calls on my machine. Four of 'em from guys. [...] I joined this video-dating thing. One's an extremely handsome, sensitive CEO who makes time for his many friends. One's in construction, but he likes long walks in the rain ... One's a Christian, and he only dates women between five-eight and six-one, which I don't think is very Christian of him, and they gotta be blonde but he'll consider a dyed blonde who accepts Jesus ... *(Thrilled)* And the last guy's a smoker. [...] Plus, he doesn't want kids, he lives in Manhattan, he likes to eat in restaurants, which is where I like to eat, and he doesn't jog. So, I figure as long as he doesn't have bad breath, a record, or a fish on his car, this is it. The bet's up in thirty days. This is the guy. [...]

Don't you want to know about the bet? [...] I'll have another. [...] See, I made a bet with my mother five years ago after I read this article she sent me from *Newsweek*. [...] The article said the odds of my getting married by forty were not quite as good as the odds of my being shot by a terrorist. I wonder how come these articles never mention the possibility of a terrorist falling madly in love and wanting to marry you? [...] So anyway, I bet my mother a hundred bucks I'd beat the odds, and I went to work. [...] I saw this modeling expert who said to divide my body in parts and go over it with a magnifying glass. Parts I could improve, I'd work on, and the rest I'd just cover up. So I started from the top. Hair, eyebrows — [...] Man, you should have seen the Visa bills. Luckily, I had a couple of boyfriends along the way who were very ... supportive, if not marriage material.

So then I went to work on my weight. I did Jenny Craig, Weight Watchers, Nutrisystem, Optifast, Jenny Craig, cocaine, and finally lipo. Then I met this writer in a bar who did an article on me and the bet for *Self* magazine, and the most beautiful thing started happening. Women all over the country started sending me donations. I got on *Oprah*, Great Expectations gave me a lifetime membership, I even got a letter from my local councilman — it was like, hey, even the government wants me to win! The Paramus Kiwanis Club wants to give me their hall for my wedding — the Vanity Fair Outlet is gonna give me a trousseau, Video Nuts is giving me and my husband a free membership, and the Taj Mahal in Atlantic City is donating the bridal suite! So now I got thirty days to find the guy, and this morning I went to the doctor ... and I got a tumor. *(Beat. Drinks.)* And that's how I'm doing.

Marvelous Shrine
by Leslie Bramm

Here is a raw snapshot of a distraught mother in crisis that explores the nature of heroism and the tragic impact of war while asking the provocative question, "If a young man dies in combat, would the hero's medals, the letter from the President, the flags, and ribbons fill the space left by a dead son?" Bobbie, the alcoholic mother of a son recently killed in combat, strains to come to terms with her son's death and takes a hard look at the stark truth behind this unanswerable question. Her understanding of how one survives this fatal blow to the human spirit is an intensely chilling and harrowing portrait that captures a mother's painful sense of loss for a child.

BOBBIE: His presence, still all over the house. The smell of his clothes, his hair in a brush, his sweet voice on the machine. I can feel all these pieces of my son ... He died without me. He suffered and died alone, all alone. Eighteen hours! That's how long my son fought to stay alive. That's how long he lay twisted and broken. That fragile body, mangled, burnt! Eighteen hours, in his pain, almost a full day, and I wasn't there. I wasn't there to hold his hands. Five hundred miles from home, where was I? And where are you? Where are you? You called. You called me on the phone. As soon as I hear it ring, I know it's you, and I know why. I answer ... I answer the phone and now my son is dead. "I regret to inform you," is that what you said? *(Beat)*

At his funeral a Major and three other Marines ... "You must be mistaken my son hasn't even shipped out yet. There must be some kind of ... You're going to bury my son? This is a mistake." The Major has dry spit in the corner of his mouth. It looks like toothpaste. He says my son's name. I think he's talking about you at first. I'm relieved. Then he repeats it, to make sure I hear. My son's death, simple as your phone call. Gritty and sweet, like the taste of toothpaste. He has dog tags in his hand. "No. No, it's not possible," I tell him, "He called, finally. He was okay. We spoke. It was peaceful." ... The Major apologizes, again. After a while I don't even hear the words. I watch his mouth. I watch the spit ... I watch him trying to wet his lips. *(Beat)*

They gave me a flag. Neatly folded ... I gave them a young man. A perfectly beautiful boy ... He burned to death ... I gave them a boy. They gave me a flag.

Yellow Dishes
by Jolene Goldenthal

Amy, a distraught and reclusive young woman, regrets that she did not take a set of yellow dishes to preserve the loving memory of her mother, who offered the dishes as a lasting memento while she lay dying. The yellow dishes with a tiny painted butterfly on the rim of each plate have since shaped Amy's identity and now become a symbol of the broken bonds of her family with the passage of time. In a quietly shattering revelation, Amy's stepmother unflinchingly reveals the truth about the dishes and severs the delicate bond between the two women.

AMY: "Take something," my mother said. "Take the china vase in the dining room ... take the silver bowl on the buffet ... take the little picture in the hall," she pleaded, fighting for breath. I wanted to please her. I wanted to do that, but I could not do it.

I knew just what I would take ... if I could. The yellow dishes. The shiny yellow dishes with a tiny painted butterfly on the rim of each plate, each cup, each bowl. I should have gone into the kitchen right then, pulled each piece off the shelves and carried them home with me.

But I couldn't. I couldn't. That would have meant admitting to myself that my mother was dying. That soon she would be gone from me. And I couldn't. *(Pause)*

Times were bad when I was a child. And then one surprising day my father found a new job. Suddenly there was money and my mother bought the yellow dishes. I was fascinated by the butterfly that sat on my breakfast cocoa cup and cereal bowl and appeared again like magic at lunch and at supper if I cleaned my plate. *(Pause)*

"Take something," my mother whispered painfully. But I didn't. I couldn't. I should have saved that part of my childhood. Of my past. Of my mother. But I could not do that. *(Pause)*

My stepmother has the yellow dishes now. I've tried to tell her what they mean to me. I've tried to ask her for them. It's not easy, but I have tried. Today I ask her again.

"Oh I know," she smiles at me. "They are pretty, aren't they? So bright. So cheerful. I gave them to my daughter. I know you understand. But, oh, wait here ... "

She hands me a small cracked bowl with a faded butterfly on the rim.

"I saved this for you," she says.

"Okay," I tell her ... "Thanks."

I take it in my hand and I begin to cry.

Stepping Stones
by Barbara Lhota

Marge, a feisty, seasoned nursery school teacher wise in the ways and wiles of four year olds, offers crucial advice to a frantic teacher new to the magical mayhem of kindergarten. Her battle-tested advice is both laughable and lucid at the same time, but with a healthy dose of reality and full of familiar hyperactive hyperbole. Marge's lesson plan for success — a survival kit really — is full of ripe earthy humor and offers a wide array of knowledge guaranteed to avoid inescapable disaster in the classroom. Armed with a generous dose of Marge's "how-to" guide book for survival, both teachers charge off to face the enemy, determined to win and keep on winning!

MARGE: Montessori? What are you crazy? They're nuts over there! All that learner-centered learning is dangerous. What you don't want is a bunch of focused four year olds. They're like a sponge. A slip of the tongue here, an insensitive comment made there, a swear word just slips out of your mouth and they repeat it. And they just don't repeat it, Belinda. They sing it. They dance it. They create a full Broadway-style production based on your swear word or your slightly insensitive, off-color comment for their parents. And then when the mother or father looks on in horror and says, "Now, where did you hear that?" the child smiles slyly and says your name and points directly at your heart. No, it's best to keep them unfocused and eating plastic car keys. The whole Farmer in the Dell debacle.

Didn't Lynn tell you? One smart aleck kid decided that it was insensitive to women and single mothers that the farmer took the wife. So she went home and told her mother who, as it turns out, was not only offended by the farmer taking the wife, but the wife taking the baby and left the poor cheese standing alone. Apparently, she's a big gorgonzola fan. So I just told her we'd make the farmer an oncologist, the wife, a partner, the baby, an adopted orphan girl from China, and the cheese, a huge mound of brie, well supported by an apple, pear, and a couple of grape friends. She was happy.

I didn't tell you this when I hired you, Belinda, but I used to work at a progressive nursery school like that and they reprimanded a child severely for calling an ellipse an oval. No, not a four year old. Two. Nearly threw him out. Or at least corrected him. In front of his mother. It was very shameful for him. They don't think he'll make it into Heath Academy now. Now, for us no child is too dumb, no lesson too short, and nothing is learned without us teaching it! Sure, we let them learn at their own pace at Stepping-Stone, but that doesn't mean we want them to outpace us. So stop that whiny can't do attitude. You gotta snap out of this, Ms. Harrison.

They want to see you soft. They want to see you buckle. But you won't! Because you're a tougher soldier than all of them put together. Sure you are. And I won't let those *ruffians* run the show! After the three p.m. wave-off, we'll huggy-wuggy them all and then order a vodka and tonic. I know times are tough and boot camp sucks, but cooperation is our only defense against these thugs. You with me, soldier? *(Gesturing toward the door)* Now, let's go dole out the finger paint, and silly putty, crack those soldiers into shape. I've got your back covered, Sister!

Miriam's Flowers
by Migdalia Cruz

Miriam, a despondent and disturbed young Puerto Rican girl from the South Bronx, New York, was abused as a child by her father and is now in mourning for her slain younger brother, Puli, who was recently murdered in a senseless street fight. In her struggle for self-acceptance, Miriam's only connection with reality is etching designs on her body with razor blades. Searching to find her way out of the dark abyss in the ever-present human quest for a connection to the great unknown, Miriam visits an empty church and is now talking to the statue of the Virgin Mary holding the crucified Christ.

MIRIAM: I'm the invisible girl, Mary ... always searching for a hole in the wall to pull myself through to get to the other side. The other side is only for me, I could see myself then. I could feel my fingertips then and the pointy pieces of skin being torn down the sides of my fingers. I could see the scars then, on the bottom of my thumbs from the Wilkinson Swords — I write on myself with them. I carve myself into my hands. And for Lent, Mary, I'll cover them with purple cloth. I keep my gloves on in church, until everybody leaves and then I come to you. To show you. *(She takes off her gloves.)* See? I show you mine and then I can touch yours ... *(She places her hands on the carved wounds of Jesus.)* They feel so fresh, Jesus. Like mine. I can smell the blood on them. Smells like violets and sweet coffee with five sugars, like Ma takes it ... *(Pause)* I'm never gonna die — not from my wounds anyway. I never go in deep and I don't make them long. I make little points that add up to a picture, a flower picture. And sometimes they're so pretty they make me cry, and I like that, 'cause when I get those tears on my hands and on my arms, they sting, and then I know I'm alive, 'cause it hurts so bad. Does that happen to you, too? *(Fade out.)*

The Eulogy
by G. L. Horton

A father and daughter relationship is highly complicated and yet genuinely poignant in its connections lost and found. But, at other times, it can be easily punctuated with unspeakable antagonism that spontaneously combusts and threatens to reveal secrets of the past. In this original, deeply affecting character sketch, a reluctant daughter faces a moral crisis when she is asked to deliver the eulogy at her father's funeral, and must come to terms with the life-shattering incidents that caused her to drift perilously apart from her father. At the same time, the daughter is forced to come to terms with a haunted past before it is too late.

DAUGHTER: When my father died all these people came up to me or sent me cards saying they felt with me in my loss. What loss? How could they? If they thought it was a loss, they didn't really know me. They didn't know him, either — or rather, they knew him the way most people knew him: the public man. Not what he was to me, not in private.

My father had so many friends. He was active in all these charities and in the town and people all thought he was so generous and charming. Not to me! I was the family scapegoat, his punching bag. But I can't say that, can I? No one would believe it. Except my sister. She's often said to me that she could never understand why my father was so cold and cruel to me. If he had behaved towards her as he did to me, she couldn't have stood it, she says. I couldn't stand it either, but what could I do?

Comes the funeral, everyone said to me, "You're creative, you're the writer, you must write something to read to the congregation." What could I write? What could I say that wouldn't be a lie? He's my father, yes. But as soon as I could I put distance between us, to put a limit to how much he could hurt me. Am I to say that? Shame the family? In the end, I went around and gathered little stories from people, about his charm and his jokes and his good deeds, and put them together as "so and so says about my father that ... " even though to me he was nothing like that. I don't think anybody noticed that it was all hearsay, not admissible in court. I didn't actually say anything in my own voice. Not a word of false witness — just a false impression, with the terrible black facts left out.

Shakespeare says "the evil that men do lives after them, the good is oft interred with their bones." But here it's the opposite. I am burying the evil, consigning it to silence. All those years in the family he must have thought that what he was doing to me was right, that he was doing the right thing according to some principle or other. He was a righteous man. Everyone said so. But what principle? When he was cruel to me, when he punished me for no reason, no one ever questioned it or confronted him. I tried, but he never explained. "You know what you've done," he'd say. But I didn't know. I don't know to this day, and no one else knows either. When I asked them they'd say, "You did nothing, you don't deserve this" — or "That's just how he is. It isn't fair but what can you do?"

At the funeral I wanted to speak up at last: to say he wasn't fair, he was terrible and cruel to me — can't any of you tell me why? You knew him. Give me some sort of explanation! I can't forgive what I don't understand! And that's the truth. I can't forgive him. But I can forget him. I have the strength. I can let my father's dark side go in silence into his grave, to be interred with his bones — and let his good live after him. Amen.

Venus
by Suzan-Lori Parks

In this sensitive meditation based on a true story about the historical ambiguity of race in early 19th century colonization, Pulitzer Prize winning playwright Suzan-Lori Parks introduces Venus, a young black woman lured away from her menial job in South Africa to tour the world as a curious novelty. Venus is, of course, paraded in front of sometimes jeering throngs and loudly ridiculed because of her origin and rather startling size. Eventually, however, her personal testament of human bravery and personal dignity shines through the bleakness and there is a momentary glimmer of hope reflected in her struggle for acceptance and respect. In this brief episode, Venus serves up a wise, witty, and worldly lecture on "A Brief History of Chocolate."

VENUS:
"A Brief History of Chocolate:"
It is written in the ancient chronicles
that the Gods one day looked down with
pity on the people as they struggled.
The Gods resolved to visit the people
and teach them the ways of Love
for love helps in times of hardship.
As an act of Love one God gives to the people
a little shrub that had, until then, belonged
only to the Gods.
This was the cacao tree.
(Rest)
Time passed.
Time passed again:
We find ourselves in the 19th century.
The Aztec word *cacao* literally "food of the Gods"
becomes *chocolate* and *cocoa*.

124

The *cacao* bean, once used as money
becomes an exotic beverage.
The Spanish were known to die for their chocolate.
In the New World, they were also known to kill for it.
In Europe the church wages a campaign against chocolate
on the grounds that it was tainted by the character
of its heathen inventors.
"Chocolate is the damnable agent of necromancers and sorcerers,"
said one French cleric circa 1620.
The pilgrims in America. Some said they fled England because of
the chocolate.
But that's another story.
(Rest)
Chocolate was soon mixed with milk and sugar
and formed into lozenges which one could eat on the run.
Chocolate lozenges are now found in a variety of shapes
mixed with everything from nuts to brandy.
Chocolate is a recognized emotional stimulant,
for doctors have recently noticed the tendency of some persons,
especially women,
to go on chocolate binges
binges either *after* emotionally upsetting incidents
or in an effort to allow themselves to *handle* an incident
which may be emotionally upsetting.
This information is interesting in that it has become the practice
to present a gift of chocolates when professing Love.
This practice, begun some time ago, continues to this day.
(Rest)
While chocolate was once used as a stimulant and source of
nutrition
it is primarily today a great source of fat,
and, of course, pleasure.
(Rest)

Love-Lies-Bleeding
by Don DeLillo

Lia, younger second wife and recent widow of an eccentric artist left invalid after a series of debilitating strokes, struggles to deliver a memorial tribute following his death. Here, she weaves a meditative, poetic, and profound eulogy about the secrets that hold families together, and the sad truths we sometimes choose to ignore in the people we love. Her words bear witness to the unforeseen and often hidden consequences of private grief while offering an unflinching look at what it truly means to be alive. Lia's feelings about human destiny, the will to live, and matters of the spirit are a sympathetic answer to the ultimate question, "How do you let a loved one die with grace and dignity?"

LIA: I don't know if it's customary for the wife to speak at a memorial service. The widow. But I came here to say that everything you may believe you know about Alex is only what you know, and it's not everything.

He was not the older man. I was not the younger woman. Can you understand that? The woman half his age, or whatever I was, or whatever he was. We never thought of each other as husband and wife. We were married but we never used those words or fit ourselves into them. I don't know what we were. We were one life, one pulse.

I understand now how two people can live together and when one of them dies, the other has to stop living. The other can't live a single day or a single week. A day may be passable, livable. A week, too long and dark. One dies, the other has to die.

I know people tell stories at these gatherings. I don't want to do that. People tell stories, exchange stories. I don't know any stories. You know things about him that I never knew. This means nothing to me. There are no stories. You're here for the wrong reason. If you're here to honor his memory, it's not his memory, it's your memory, and it's false. There are no stories. There are other things, hard to express, so deep and true that I can't share them, and don't want to. In the end it's not what kind of man he was but simply that he's gone. The stark fact. The thing that turns us into children, alone under the sky. When it stops being unbearable, it becomes something worse. It becomes the air we breathe. My failure came at the end. He could have gone on, I could not. My weakness, my failure, this is what I carry. His life is what I carry, step by step. He left in the arms of Morpheus, god of dreams. I've come all this way to say these things.

You'll leave and forget what I've said and so will I. I'll go back home and climb into the burning hills, where he worked, and scatter his ashes there. He goes nowhere now, into nothing. What powerful work he had it in mind to make. Untitled, unfinished. But not nothing.

Etiquette and Vitriol
by Nicky Silver

There is a very fine — if not invisible — line between fantasy and reality and between normal and abnormal. This excerpt crosses both those anguished lines with genuine hilarity and the end itself, like life, is a splendid and invigorating awareness that those who are unable to confront the demons of their past are doomed forever. Bishop, an introverted young man with a severe stuttering problem, and his mother are stranded on a deserted island for five years after a plane crash. What transpires during those lost years is unspeakable! There are, however, echoes of mayhem, savagery, and cannibalism not easily silenced when mother and son are later rescued. Now haunted by his mother's ghost, Bishop is being treated in a hospital for the criminally insane and pursued by a demonically cheerful fellow inmate named Popo. Here, the witty Popo introduces herself with all the shiny humor that escapes from her distorted world of illusion.

POPO: I am Popo Martin. My friends call me Popo Martin. Dr. Nestor says I'm a paranoid schizophrenic. I think I have Marnie's disease. You know, like Tippi Hedren in that movie. When I see red, I see red! I mean, I have an episode. Although sometimes it happens when I don't see red. And sometimes I see red and it doesn't happen. I am the most popular girl in the hospital. I gets lots of visitors! I was a cheerleader. I'd do a cheer for you now, but I don't have my pompoms.

All my teachers love me. The girls on the squad come to visit me every Sunday. The principal sent me a get-well note and the boys autographed a football. You can ask anyone in school about me, and they'd all say the same thing. Popo Martin is always cheerful. Popo Martin is a natural leader. Popo Martin looks on the bright side. Popo Martin has a smile on her lips and a kind word for a saddened stranger. Which is probably why everyone was so surprised when it happened. I tried to kill myself! I took thirty-five sleeping pills out of my mother's purse. I didn't want to smile anymore. My jaw hurts. And whistling gives me a headache. I want, more than anything, to wallow in a hopeless depression but it just goes against my grain. So I tried to kill myself. That's why I'm here.

Open Water
by David Moberg

This fast-paced comic duo scene about strange goings-on at a small town police headquarters deals with events as antic as they are original: Two women — She and Her — sitting nervously in a quiet, stark interrogation room dressed in the same style clothes, carry identical purses, wear the same decorative accessories, use similar gestures, and even tend to sit in similar positions ... or do they? Grappling with an answer to this real or imagined wackiness — or comic fate — and trying to unravel the fascinating mystery which accounts for such a chance encounter becomes increasingly more blurred until we are left still laughing, and simply come to terms with the reality that these characters will live happily ever after and we are powerless to do anything about it!

She and Her give a number of early, thinly veiled clues in their one-liners and withering put-downs that telescope the surprise ending and, although throats are cut with casual charm, the women do form a lovable bond of acceptance and understanding. Even the salvo of personal insults takes no prisoners or results in any casualties as the women reconcile their similarities, and boldly continue to follow the same paths in life — leaving others to settle back into the uneventful and, perhaps, unbearable routine that has become their *way of life.*

(As the scene opens, both women are sitting in chairs and it is obvious that they are stealing glances without the other one seeing.)

SHE: March twelve, 1989. Our wedding day.

HER: Really? March twelve, 1990. Our wedding day.

SHE: No wonder he missed our anniversary.

HER: He missed our anniversary every year.

SHE: Every year. In 1991 ...

HER: 1992 ...

SHE: And 1993. Three March twelves. You don't think ...

HER: And 1986, '87, and '88 for that matter.

SHE: That would make eight March twelves total.

HER: March twelve was his very favorite day of the year.

SHE: Eight March 12s. I can't believe it. I just can't believe it. I mean, there could be six more of you out there.

HER: Six more of *you*, you mean.

SHE: There's eight of us? I feel like such a Xerox.

HER: I just want to kill him ... eight times. One time for each wife.

SHE: He's probably one of those horny toads.

HER: He's a dog.

SHE: A rat.

HER: A snake.

SHE: A yellow bellied lizard.

HER: There's laws against what he's done. After I tell that detective what he's done, he's going to find himself in prison forever — married to eight *men*.

SHE: We'd never see him again?

HER: You'd want to? He's nothing but a dirty diesel smelling fox ...

SHE: A sneaking around eight-timing coyote.

HER: A lying greasy handed motor monkey.

SHE: But he is my husband.

HER: He's *my* husband.

SHE: Mine! I'm his first wife.

HER: Really?

SHE: The only one he truly cared about ...

HER: Uh-huh.

SHE: He used to tell me over and over ...

HER: That all the other women he was married to really didn't mean anything to him.

SHE: He used to tell me over and over ... he'd say that I was his ... *(HER finishes the lines with SHE.)*

HER and SHE: Sweetest like sugar cookie.

HER: And that he ...

HER and SHE: Never met a chocolate chip cookie with so many chips.

HER: And every night when he'd come home, he'd ...

SHE: Toss his truck driving gloves over ...

HER: His left shoulder so they'd

SHE: Leave a diesel stain against the "Home Sweet Home" needlepoint

HER: Hanging on the door ...

SHE: Then grab me around the waist ...

HER: Swing me one and a half times to the sofa ...

SHE and HER: Green brocade Sears Home Life special sale ...

SHE: Set me gently down ...

SHE and HER: *"never put them sweet little Twinkies on the cushions, Darling!"*

HER: Grab the compact disc player remote ...

SHE: Click to disc four ...

HER: Track five ...

SHE: Then rush back to the sofa singing ...

HER and SHE: *(Singing)* "I ain't nothing but a hound dog, a howling all the time." *(Pause)*

SHE: That semi-stinking skunk.

HER: Eighteen-wheeled toad.

SHE: Over-sexed road hog.

HER: I really hate that song.

SHE: I'm going to mash peanut butter cookies into those sofa cushions.

HER: I'm never buying another Keebler cookie again.

SHE: He said his mother made that "Home Sweet Home" needlepoint specially for me.

HER: K-Mart, the arts and craft section, pre-framed for a dollar and ninety-seven cents.

SHE: *(Standing and indicating her dress)* He said he special ordered *this* from Burdines.

HER: *(Flat without emotion)* Wal-Mart. Nineteen ninety-five, ten percent off on a purchase of five or more.

SHE: *(Holding up her purse)* A present from last Christmas, a genuine alligator purse hemmed together by a real Seminole Indian.

HER: *(Holding up identical purse)* Bulk buy. Mail order. Made in Taiwan.

SHE: *(She slumps, deflated and dejected, not looking at anyone.)* He's such a ...

HER: *(Finishing her sentence)* Love sucking insect.

SHE: I could just ...

HER: Squash him like a blooded bloated mosquito.

SHE: And mash his face into the pavement ...

HER: Like ripe road kill on hot asphalt.

SHE: This really ...

HER and SHE: Sucks. *(They both sit for a moment, stunned by the realization of their shared dilemma.)*

SHE: Well, like my husband always says, "Diesel doesn't stink, darling ...

HER: *(Finishing the sentence)* If you pull your nose out of the tank." I hate his diesel philosophy.

SHE: Well, it's true. Let's just try to make do. I'm Betty. *(She extends her hand.)*

HER: Really? I'm Betty, too. I mean Betty also.

SHE: And my last name is ...

HER: Smith. I know.

SHE: Oh. What's yours?

HER: What?

SHE: Your last name?

HER: *(A bit irritated)* Smith.

SHE: Oh. Right. Yeah. And I live at 1212 Rainbow Lane Southwest.

HER: 1212 Rainbow Lane Southeast.

SHE: Oh, that two-story peach painted Jim Walter's home with white trim and shutters? Why that house looks ...

HER: Just like yours. Go figure.

SHE: Why, yes it does! Even your oak trees are planted in the same place. I've just got to know, we've got that off-white tan flecked berber-barbour carpet in every room except the kitchen ...

131

HER: So do we …

SHE: Of course I said, "White carpet, Honey? In every single room. You really want every room the same?" And besides, I said, "White carpet shows every itty bitty fleck of dirt and dog hair … "

HER: You have a dog?

SHE: A terrier, black and white …

HER: Mostly spotted …

SHE: And her name is …

BOTH: Oriolo.

SHE: Anyway, he insisted on white. Besides the green sofa …

HER: And brown suede chair?

SHE: And matching early American Oak end tables and —

BOTH: Clear glass seashell lamps …

SHE: Will match perfectly.

HER: Well, they do. I'll give him that.

SHE: But keeping that front entryway clean, particularly when he leaves his boots there …

HER: The high top brown ones with …

BOTH: Orange New York Met laces.

SHE: You know the first time he tracked diesel on my white carpet …

HER: I just about killed him … "Honey," … I said …

SHE: "Our house is not the rear end of your semi truck."

HER: And he said.

SHE: "I'm sorrier than a melted butterscotch cookie."

HER: Yes, he did.

SHE: And he was.

HER: Down on his knees he got and scrubbed that carpet …

SHE: With Ajax …

HER: Until every drop of that diesel was white and gone.

SHE: Yes he did.

HER: Such a hard worker …

SHE: And courteous …

HER: Thoughtful.

SHE: Do you know when my dishwasher clogged …

HER: A Kenmore?

SHE: Triple cycle soap saver …

HER: Antique enamel white?

SHE: Absolutely. Has to be to match oyster countertops …
HER: And seashell kitchen wallpaper.
SHE: The man has fabulous decorating taste.
HER: Impeccable.
SHE: Just the best.
HER: And an eye for color … Do you know that shower curtain in the master bath …
SHE: Mint green with oyster accents …
HER: Coordinates perfectly with the twill patterned bedspread …
SHE: And matching valances.
HER: The eye of a Da Vinci.
SHE: Sees form like Picasso.
HER: Mixes texture like Monet.
SHE: He sees the world like an —
HER: Artist.
SHE: Talks like a —
HER: Poet.
SHE: Treats me like I'm the …
BOTH: *Queen of the world! (A Pause. They both realize what they have just said.)*
HER: He does?
SHE: Like the princess of the whole universe. He's only home about one night a week, but like he always says …
BOTH: *"Out of every seven, we spend one night in heaven!"*
SHE: He's so …
HER: Gently sensuous …
SHE: So …
HER: Lovingly considerate …
SHE: And he's always an …
BOTH: *Animal! (Both women sigh a very satisfied sigh as they recall the passion moments. There is another brief pause.)*
HER: Betty?
SHE: *(Still lost in thought and passion.)* Yes, Betty?
HER: What if …
SHE: What if what?
HER: Well, tomorrow Sears is delivering my new fabric sensing washing machine …

SHE: And the new touch-plate low heat dryer? Mine came yesterday, and what a difference it makes for those hand-washed silk blend sweaters.

HER: The purple and beige sweaters didn't fade on your pink pattern bra?

SHE: It's a Kenmore ... need I say more?

HER: You know, he's only home on Tuesday.

SHE: Thursday for me.

HER: And he's always well-groomed ...

SHE: Arid extra dry and no grease under the fingernails.

HER: And the rest of the time I ... I mean, *we* have to ourselves. We have a beautiful house ...

SHE: Beautifully furnished ...

HER: A dog ...

SHE: Adequately trained ...

HER: A two-car garage ...

SHE: With two cars in it.

HER: And one husband ...

SHE: Only one night a week.

HER: No meals to cook.

SHE: Dirty socks soaking ...

HER: Screaming relatives ...

SHE: Bad breath morning.

HER: Think about it. He's really ...

SHE: An excellent provider ...

HER: A concerned and thoughtful mate ...

SHE: A generous gift-giving man.

HER: Annnnd —

BOTH: *Out of every seven, one night in heaven!*

HER: What time is it, Betty?

SHE: About four thirty p.m.

HER: Hmmmm. It's four thirty p.m. in the afternoon on a Tuesday. *My* hungry husband will be coming through the front door at five thirty p.m. sharp, humming some dumb Elvis tune and looking for his country fried steak and steamed tomatoes. *(Pause. The two women stare into each other's eyes. Her stands.)* I really can't be wasting my afternoon sitting around any police station. *(Starts to leave.)*

Are you staying or coming? *("SHE" pauses and stares intently at "HER.")*

SHE: You know, *my* husband will be home day after tomorrow, and I have a house to clean, corn bread muffins to bake, and a spotted dog to walk. I can't be sitting around here either. *(They start to leave.)*

HER: I only cook with low fat oil.

SHE: And no salt …

HER: Even though he complains about it.

SHE: Any plans for Friday?

HER: None, he's gone for the weekend.

SHE: Lunch Friday at my house?

HER: Love to! *(They exit arm in arm.)*

CHAPTER 6
SONGS OF RAGE AND RETRIBUTION

"one thing I don't need
is any more apologies
i got sorry greetin me at my front door
you can keep yrs
i don't know what to do wit em
they don't open doors
or bring the sun back
they don't make me happy
or get a morning paper
didn't nobody stop usin my tears to wash cars
cuz a sorry"
— Ntozake Shange, *For colored girls who have considered*
suicide/when the rainbow is enuf

These vignettes examine the sometimes comic or tragic trials and tribulations of characters who seek revenge on others by telling the "truth," even if it means terrible consequences. The difference between a hurtful truth and an expedient lie, however, ironically becomes the means of each character's undoing. Characters probe into the dark corners of their own lives and offer harrowing, satiric, or personal hymns that emerge from their self-inflicted agony and rage that cuts to the bone.

Although solitary figures for the most part, at times the characters reveal a genuine sense of humor and humanity. For the most part, however, they are held prisoner by personal yearnings that cannot be repressed. They cry out for help, but one by one each disparate soul can only lament the failure and frustration that shook the foundation of their faith, spirit, morality, or need for human companionship. It is this sense of frailty and infirmity that make them less than they want to be in the eyes and hearts of others.

In these monologues and duo scenes, there are gossamer tales of love and trickery, caustic doses of anger and angst, delicate distortions of memory and truth, and a keen eye for poking fun at the absurdity of life. There are themes that explore fate, heroic misadventures, tragic flaws, failed romances, and moral or social issues. There is also a smug refrain that suggests the need for acceptance and courage to straighten out the mayhem still churning in its wake with what little is left of each character's life.

Happily or unhappily, these fractured lives fall back into place when the characters inevitably experience that moment of truth that teaches a sobering lesson about evildoers who earn their just deserts, while the virtuous are rewarded and triumphant. In spite of the most ludicrous outbursts, unexpected obstacles, or hopeless confrontations they endured, the characters sing their delicately poetic and intriguing songs but somehow manage to emerge at the end none the worse. They resolve to live their lives another day and move on from disturbing memories to better hopes for what lies ahead ... or simply slip deeper into depression and despair.

Role Play

In playing these familiar characters it is important to design an audition blueprint that suggests "a picture of reality," not reality itself. Each character's physical activity, vocal quality, and movement should suggest a self-portrait that may have been snapped by a handheld camera to capture an authentic everyday person. There should be no theatrical tricks, artificial posing, or any attempt to distort the character portrait depicted in everyday observations of life.

Remember that it is the *subtext* — or hidden meaning of a character's thought that lies just beneath the surface of the language — that should convey the verbal or emotional tug-of-war between what a character says and what is actually meant. So pay special attention to fragmented sentences, broken phrases, incomplete thoughts, or extended moments of silence that may reveal a character's point of view or provide audition performance insights.

Approach each monologue and duo scene with sensitivity and strive for a conversational tone of delivery, relaxed and natural sense of movement, and energy that highlights a singleness of purpose. "Subtle" and "suggestive" are the key words to keep in mind in both the rehearsal period and in an audition. It may be helpful to integrate the dress of realism — blouses, leisure skirts, pantsuit, or slacks — to more clearly define your character.

It will also be important during the rehearsal period to conceal the more obvious mechanics of your acting technique and focus on a natural and spontaneous *self*-expression. Concentrate on a single performance objective for each character's action, intention, and motivation in order to personalize the story being described in the script. Focus attention on character attitude or behavior to reveal idiosyncrasies or behavioral traits as well.

This more "illustrative" approach to character building is essential in giving a personal life and meaning to the given circumstances of the text, as well as to more clearly define character actions or reactions. Skillful use of an occasional hand prop to enrich the portrait may also define a character's personality traits or mannerisms. The most important audition principle to keep in mind, however, is to paint an honest and believable character portrait that any observer could easily recognize — and just as easily identify in their own life experiences.

Stamping, Shouting and Singing Home
by Lisa Evans

This somber character sketch challenges our assumptions about race and individual dignity. Marguerite, a strong-willed young woman, paints an unnerving and still provocative portrait of everyday injustices reserved for African Americans in the Deep South of the 1950s. Here she describes for her mother and younger sister, Lizzie, what happens when she attempts to eat at a local café reserved for "Whites Only" and refuses to give in to second-rate treatment at a café. Although her story is a heartbreaking narrative of recent American history, it is also an ode to the strength of individual freedom and the power to effect meaningful social change.

MARGUERITE: I didn't plan on staying out late Mama. It was light when I went in. It was real crowded but only a few folks sitting outside at them pretty tables on the sidewalk. So I went and sat there too. Folks were staring like I come from Mars or some place. You think my skin green not brown. But I didn't take notice. I sat at the table and waited for the waitress. Pretty soon she come out and took an order from the table next to mine. Then she goes back inside. Through the glass I could see white folks nudging and laughing at me, and the waitress talking to the manager. She come out with the order for the next table. This time I say, "Excuse me, Miss." But she act like I wasn't there. No voice. No sound. But I heard my voice. And I heard it again when next she pass and I say, very polite, "I'd like a cup of coffee, please." I ask three more times but she carries on acting like I'm invisible.

Then it come on to rain. But I sat on. I sat on while it got dark and they turned up the lights inside. And folks came and went and had coffee and cake and talked and laughed together. And I sat on. Pretending I didn't care. They weren't going to drive me away. Flood could have come and I'd have stayed, sitting in the dark, rain on the window panes, running down my back till I didn't rightly know if I was turned to stone. Some cars hooted as they drove off, laughing and yelling foul words. But I sat on. I had a right to be sitting there. I had a right to be served coffee just like they did. So I sat on. Then they closed up, put out the lights. I got up and come home.

Through a Cloud
by Jack Shepherd

Although set in England during the mid-1600s of the Commonwealth period when a sad and disillusioned Oliver Cromwell is being courted to become king, there is a contemporary flavor about this monologue that calls into question the jaded aspirations of those in power and those who choose to sit in silence on the sidelines. Katherine Woodstock, feisty wife of the poet John Milton, however, is not the silent type. When she speaks of animals feeling the same happiness and misery as mortals, a sudden hush falls over the picnic lunch being served as guests are stunned by this heretical outburst, which not so long ago would have been an admission of heresy and sent her to the stake for burning.

KATHERINE: Happiness is so short-lived, isn't it? And so is misery, thank goodness. If you're sad one day, it doesn't mean to say you won't be happy the next. Yesterday, down by the river, I saw a kingfisher perched on a pole. Its feathers were still wet from skimming over the water and diving down for fish. Such a beautiful bird. I wanted to hold it. Feel its beating heart. But when I got too close, it flew away in a dazzle of blue. *(She lays three places on the grass. Each one with plate, knife, beaker, and napkin.)*

What makes us so special, Mr. Cromwell? Who's to say the birds and the animals don't feel just like we do. And the insects too ... Joy. Hunger. Hope and despair. Who's to say? *(Silence)*

When I was a little girl, I was told by our minister that animals didn't have souls. That only *we* have souls, we humans. And it upset me terribly. Aren't they mortal, too, I thought, just like we are? What makes us so special that God should single us out for immortality and not the rest of his creation? And for a while, I'm afraid to say, I lost my faith. It was not until I started to believe ... Secretly believe ... that the rest of God's creatures must have souls as well ... that my faith began to return. And everything started to feel whole again ... It's what I believed then. When I was young and innocent. But I'm a grown woman now. And I know how things go in the world.

Foreign Bodies
by Susan Yankowitz

Sarah, an independent and thoughtful teenage daughter of a corporate lawyer, is devastated in this original monologue when she learns her father is working pro bono *to defend a killer who has brutally murdered a number of prostitutes. She refuses to suppress her feelings and confronts her father while laying down the law in her own uncertain terms. As she wrestles with the frustration of the moment, Sarah's temperament ranges from fierce indignation to unabashed anger and she questions why and how her father could possibly sacrifice his honor, dignity, and reputation to publicly defend such a vile and vicious predator. The verbal confrontation is as much a debate about the struggle of independence as it is about the need for justice that gives us a way to honor our beliefs as well as ourselves.*

140

SARAH: How can you do it, Dad, how can you justify it? I'm so ashamed I could die. My own father taking sides with a sickie like that, my own father! And you never told me! Sure, people have to get defended, sure they have their constitutional rights, but you don't have to be the one, you don't have to defend a scumbag who cuts women into pieces and dumps them in the river! How would you feel if it's because of you he gets off and into the streets again? How do you know I won't be the next one he grabs? Because it could be anyone, me or Kate or even Mom, even Mom. One was a teenager, just like me; you know that and you don't care. You just want to have your name in the paper; you want to be on the news. Well, I saw your name in the paper today and all my friends saw it, too, and they think there's something wrong with you, they think it's disgusting you're defending him. And so do I. You're going to sit in the same room with that guy day after day, for months, maybe, and don't you think it rubs off on you, the way he thinks, the way he feels, don't you think it will infect you? Well, it will, you can't escape it, you'll come home at night and you'll kiss me and smell of him, and of lies and blood and his filthy hands on those poor women, those poor women reeled out of the river stinking like fish and you're bringing that into my home and Mom's home, and you're my father. My father! How can you look at yourself in the mirror? How? I can't look at you! I'll never be able to look at you again!

Phat Girls
by Debbie Lamedman

A troubled young girl, the Compulsive Overeater, struggles with an eating disorder and low self-esteem issues in an heroic attempt to triumph over a cruel stereotype that has condemned her to a hellish private world of shameless guilt. In this suspenseful confrontation with a sympathetic friend, the young girl is forced to turn her eyes upon herself and come face to face, at last, with a bitter and inevitable reality. In a climax that is both surprising and a startling cry for help, the Compulsive Overeater is able to place the blame where it truly belongs. Perhaps the ultimate lesson here is the need for compassion and understanding in judging those whose lifestyle and self-image may differ from our own.

COMPULSIVE OVEREATER: *(Overwhelmed)* No, I don't want to get on the scale and see how much I've gained. You think getting on the scale is going to motivate me to lose? You've obviously never had my problem. I don't even own a scale. I know when I'm packing on the pounds — I can tell by the way my clothes fit. And if I go into major denial and just wear sweats all the time, like *now,* I still know I'm getting fat ... ya know how I know? When I can't reach over my own gut to cut my toenails. Hey man — that's fat! When it starts to become too hard to wipe my own ... That's when I know that I've gone too far. Oh, I'm sorry. Have I shocked you? Is that too graphic for ya? Too much information? Well, welcome to my world!

These are the things nobody ever talks about. I love it when people tell me all I have to do is join a gym or lay off the sweets — it's no big deal, just do it already and stop complaining about it. Well I say try telling an alcoholic to quit mixing the martinis and downing the tall boys! Try telling a smoker to lay off the cigs for a day. They'll laugh in your face. They'll say they don't have a problem. They're not *addicted!* This is my fix. Food. And I can't seem to stop! I'm outta control and I know it and I want to do something about it but I can't seem to stop! And you can't help me. I know that now. No one can help me. No one can do this, but me.

Sister Santa
by Jim Chevallier

In this original dark and yet delightful parody of the glittering yuletide season, Sister Santa is a sour holiday elf who betrays sacred holiday myths with explosive humor and a wild spirit of adventure. There are no warm moments of holiday cheer or yuletide songs here as Sister Santa hands out one gift-wrapped insult after another and taunts the startled children standing impatiently in line for a glimpse of jolly old Saint Nick. There is an infectious and refreshing comic touch here as well, and it's clear that the young children have learned a new awareness of the ways of the world. Although hardly the richer, they are certainly the wiser for their experience — with, perhaps, the promise of quieter and happier holidays later to come. Bah, Humbug!

SISTER SANTA: Ho, ho, ho!

I am too Santa Claus, kid. Yeah, I'm a girl. Like duh-uh. Because I need the money, OK? It's either you little germ-donors or cooking Christmas burgers at the local take-out.

Hey, but enough about me. What greedy little totally unreasonable demand do you want to make of the Great White Beard? No, I didn't grow the beard. I'm a girl, OK? We don't as a general thing grow beards. Hey, look, would you rather have me or some red-eyed wino who's working off his last bottle of Boone's Farm? Like liquor-breath, do you? Well, then, work with me here, OK? I got midterms next week plus a female problem you don't want to know about, so trust me, I am not in the mood.

What'll it be then? A molded plastic semi-automatic so you can imitate your favorite mad gunman? Some bloodthirsty boy-doll that crawls around on its belly, armed to the teeth? A little remote control tank you can send shooting through pedestrians' feet and scare the Pampers off frail old ladies? Come on, sweetie, you just tell Sister Santa here what violence and mayhem disguised as a toy will put your little testosterone-tainted heart all a flutter. Rat-a-tat-tat! Boom, boom, boom!

No, I do *not* have a problem with men! Where do you get this stuff? What kind of shows do your parents let you watch, anyway? And no there is nothing weird about a female Santa! You better get used to it, kid, when you grow up, there's gonna be girls *everywhere!* Yeah, that's right, we're even in the Army!

Ah no, now I've gone and made you cry. Hey, can we get a nurturer over here?

Anyone into being maternal?

Geez …

143

Cutting Remarks
by Barbara Lhota

Candie, a grumpy kindergarten teacher, quickly accelerates to a fit of near hysteria when she innocently strikes up a conversation with Dana, a recently fired stranger she happens to meet at a local hair salon. Although Dana remains calm about her own sad circumstances, Candie's unnerving verbal assault on people who are concerned about our educational system, and increasingly place the blame on teachers, is much more frightening. Candie's cynical tirade bears witness to the often hidden testimony of how the other half lives in the teaching profession — and explores how their lives have been changed more than they would have the desire or, perhaps, the courage to admit.

CANDIE: They always want to blame the teachers. *(Looking up)* But what about the parents? It's always that *we're* incompetent. *We're* overpaid. *We* need more education. What about the parents? They don't need an education? They can be dumb as bricks. Half my students come in and they don't even know their real name, let alone how to spell it. *(Kid voice)* "I don't know my name. My momma calls me Fifi." More than half us teachers have two degrees. I only have one, but I was a straight-A student. Well, three Bs and a D in physics, but those were dumb classes. And that's not the point. I plan to go to grad school! Once I pay off undergrad. Twelve million years from now. "Oh, get educated on soft subjects like sympathetic behavior." What about a little sympathy toward us? We're stuck with your brats every day! *(Tosses down her magazine.)* I read articles on this "No Child Left Behind" stuff and get all worked up. Sure, it's good to focus on education, watch out for kids, but I have been doing this for a while now, and not just kindergarten, and let me tell you, there are some children we should leave behind. If we don't, they'll teach the others and take over. In fact, there's at least two I'd like to ship off to Canada.

Whalesong in My Latte
by Jennifer DiMarco

This comic gem doesn't provide enough rest periods between gentle laughs and gleeful winks. It features a stage-struck young actress who bubbles along with a delicious assortment of irresistible charm and showbiz ambition. She lives life according to her own free spirit and is not influenced by other people's rules. All is blissful in her dream world as she imagines herself becoming one of the most ingenious artists of our time. Here, she gives us a true thespian's message of faith, hope, and charity in a way that cannot be expressed with more hilarity than when she breaks into an animated "whale song" to punctuate her exit stage left!

ACTRESS: There's this woman in Seattle who for a hundred and fifty bucks will write you a three-minute monologue guaranteed to land you a job. For twenty bucks more she'll read your palm and bless your favorite loafers.

Not that I need anything like that. I'm a professional actress. Have been since I was six. On three — *separate* —occasions I've been paid. I've had numerous successes — third teeny-bopper to the left in the KFC national leaps to mind — but the highlight of my career was doing "Shakespeare in the Raw" with Sylvester Stallone in the kiddy pool at Lincoln Park. Oh, it was so indie. We performed sixteen hours a day for six days. At one point an *entire* Girl Scout troop was in the audience. That's like ten people. When the cops finally showed we'd already made an impact. The *Weekly* said we "did things to Shakespeare that no one has done before." Isn't that intense?

Anyway, in the life of any great artiste there are staggering highs and humbling — but short lived! — lows. Right now I'm living with my mom ... on the couch. She turned my old room into a bird aviary. I had a great place on Capital Hill with my boyfriend but he got cast as Doon in "Brigadoon" and said he needed some space to connect with his inner Scot. Whatever.

So just for a lark, you know, I took out a personal loan — twenty-eight-point-eight percent interest plus collateral — my '73 VW Bug —

and I went to see Madam Hollywood — you know, the chick who writes monologues? I plopped down my cash and five minutes later she's done. "Whalesong." That's my monologue.

Honestly? It's incredible. It's the best thing I've ever read — and I've read every play at the West Seattle library. It's so ... true. So deep. I mean really *deep*. When I'm done here I've got an audition at the Woodland Park Aquarium. Voice over. A national. I'm confident. *(Breaks into extended whalesong.)*

August: Osage County
by Tracy Letts

Violet, the acidic and pill-popping mother figure of the Osage County, Oklahoma, Weston clan is the center of attention in this Pulitzer Prize drama that exposes the dark side of a near-apocalyptic Midwestern family meltdown. With nostrils flaring and fangs bared, Violet hosts a life-and-death family reunion after her husband disappears — and the homestead is literally set ablaze in a firestorm of squashed dreams, resentful truths, and repressed secrets that threaten to erupt in violence at any moment. The characters struggle to make sense of their dysfunctional lives by turning upon each other as they each come to terms with the tortured past.

VIOLET: I ever tell you the story of Raymond Qualls? Not much story to it. Boy I had a crush on when I was thirteen or so. Real rough-looking boy, beat up Levis, messy hair. Terrible under-bite. But he had these beautiful cowboy boots, shiny chocolate leather. He was so proud of those boots, you could tell, the way he'd strut around, all arms and elbows, puffed up and cocksure. I decided I needed to get a girly pair of those same boots and I knew he'd ask me to go steady, convinced myself of it. He'd see me in those boots and say, "Now there's the gal for me." Found the boots in a window downtown and just went crazy: I'd stay up late in bed, rehearsing the conversation I was going to have with Raymond when he saw me in my boots. Must've asked Momma a hundred times if I could get those boots. "What do you want for Christmas, Vi?" "Momma, I'll give all of it up for those boots."

146

Bargaining, you know? She started dropping hints about a package under the tree she had wrapped up, about the size of a boot box, real nice wrapping paper. "Now Vi, don't you cheat and look in there before Christmas morning." Little smile on her face. Christmas morning, I was up like a shot, boy, under the tree, tearing open that box. There was a pair of boots, all right ... men's work boots, holes in the toes, chewed up laces, caked in mud and dog poo. Lord, my Momma laughed for days. My Momma was a mean, nasty old woman. I suppose that's where I got it from.

Of Course They Call It a Tragedy
by Gus Edwards

Betsey Mae, a serious and self-confident African American woman in her late twenties, offers a captivating examination of the assassination of Dr. Martin Luther King. Here, she recalls coming of age at that precise historical moment when youthful dreams of faith and hope faded into morning-after realities of anger, dejection, and despair. Her emotion-charged outburst raises profound, unanswered questions that hold little hope of reconciliation or a deeper, fuller understanding of the national tragedy that can still divide as well as separate a people and a nation as we each struggle to make sense of our changing world.

BETSEY MAE: They were searching for a killer, they said. Sure they were. That's exactly who they were eager to find, right. The man who killed the man they were calling "The Enemy of America," forget that he had whites following him and agreeing with what it was he was preaching. Forget that he had won the Nobel Prize for peace. Forget that he said, "I have a dream that is deeply rooted in the American Dream." Those things were only making them hate him more. Do they seriously want me to believe that the F.B.I. wasn't secretly happy when they heard that he had been shot? That J. Edgar Hoover, that great defender of American democracy, wasn't in some room laughing his head off when he got the news. And that many folks all over the North and South wasn't holding secret parties because this thorn in their side

147

had been removed in the most effective way a person can be removed. With a bullet in the face.

Of course they called it a tragedy. And of course they were looking for the man who pulled the trigger. They were searching the cities and scouring the countryside with every resource they had. And with one prayer in their hearts, "Oh God, don't let it be a white man. Let it be one of their own. Some eye-rolling, rabid-looking black loony spouting quotes from Nietzsche and the Koran while waving a pistol in the air." He would of course have to be subdued with about thirty bullets through the heart. Then all would be right with America once more.

They had gotten lucky with Malcolm. It was black men who had done the deed. And perhaps this time, if they prayed hard enough. Maybe — just maybe, lightning might strike twice in the same spot again. And you want me to love you all? Think of you as nice people? Yeah. *(She laughs and exits.)*

The Eros Trilogy
by Nicky Silver

Claire, an attractive and sophisticated woman of impeccable taste and decorum, lives by her own rules and what she may lack in real-world facts, she makes up in an amazingly misguided intuition about life and people. Seated at her elaborate armoire powdering her face, Claire reflects on a distressing recent incident she observed that has punctuated her long-held belief of a serious social problem: The old ways are being trampled by the new. Speaking quite candidly, she now delivers an incisive — and hilarious — indictment on the current practice of spitting on public streets. She is unflinching in her social and moral outrage, exploring some of its more disruptive aspects, and calls attention to the chaos that ensues when civilized duties succumb to primitive desires.

CLAIRE: I have, for a long time, been a person who tries to see the best in others. I have always tried to see the beauty in all things. No matter how *grotesque*. And I find, more and more, I live in a grotesque world. Isn't everything ugly all of a sudden? I do not understand, I must admit, what passes for music in this age. But then, I force myself to remember that my mother did not understand my music, and I try to see the beauty in giving in, giving way, like a weeping willow bending gracefully in the inevitable face of gravity. *(She glances into the mirror and is momentarily side-tracked.)*

My mother was a sad woman to begin with, and then, when I was eight years old, she lost a baby. And her sadness became exaggerated to the point of farce. *(Returning to her point.)*

This morning, I went to the dressmaker, to be fitted for a dress. I walked to the shop. It's not very far and I enjoy what's left of the fresh air. And I enjoy seeing people. Or I did. You see, more and more people seem to feel it all right to behave anyway they choose. For instance, more and more people seem to be — how shall I put this? — *Spitting.* I do not approve of this. Sometimes they walk over to the curb and spit into the street, as if this were so much better than spitting in the middle of the pavement. It's not. And apparently plenty of people feel as I do and they spit right where they are. And not just men, but women too! With hairdos and skirts. Now, I want to see the beauty in all of this, but it's *very* hard. It is eight blocks from my door to the dress-maker's and I must've passed thirty-five people spitting in the first three. Is there something in the air? Is it a by-product of auto exhaust that has everyone spitting so continually? Now, I am willing to blame an awful lot on the industrial revolution, but not this, this sudden spitting frenzy. No.

Bludgeon the Lime
by Michael Weems

Ruby, a serious and spunky young girl determined to follow her own path no matter where it may lead, holds a mirror up to life as she reflects on the stormy relationship of her parents — a telling chronicle of what is right and wrong about the marriage myth "happily ever after." She dutifully probes the compassion, cynicism, and disillusionment that has ensnarled her parents as their conflicting dreams collided in a catastrophic explosion ... searing them all forever. Ruby's unflinching view in trying to straighten out the mayhem that surrounds her is, of course, taking the first sure step toward a life, which will be of her own making.

RUBY: Thanksgiving with Dad. He can't cook for beans, so we'll go out to some nice restaurant and before the napkin's on my lap he's digging for dirt and cursing Mom. We hang stockings and trim the tree. Every time I'll try to put up an old ornament I made in kindergarten of Dad dressed as Santa and me on his lap. I think I asked for a pony. *(Sigh)* I ask for a pony every year. Never got the stupid thing either. So I'll try to put it up and remind Mom that it was a memory of before things happened and that he'll always be my Dad. And of course she'll smile and nod and come Christmas morning the picture has mysteriously disappeared. Again. I'll dig it out from the same old drawer where she keeps the little things he left behind — cuff links, cigar box, my ornament — things she can't bring herself to throw away. Like he'll come back wanting them, realize what a mistake he's made, and life is peachy all over again.

I want them to be happy. You know? Stop living in the past and move on. Find someone new. It's that fear of failure and rejection that keeps them living such an insecure existence. I'm sure it's doing wonders on my subconscious.

Unbroken Heart
by Scot Walker

This sobering but inspiring original monologue builds in intensity as it probes the redemption of Peg, a young woman who was brutally assaulted as a child — but who is now determined to break free of that nightmare evening while silencing her memories of pain and suffering. On Christmas Eve, Peg comes to terms with the ghosts of the past that shattered her childhood dreams, and in the process acknowledges the right to lead her own life. There is dark at the top of everyone's stairs ... but if the spirit is undaunted, the shining light of hope, renewal, and recovery are sure to come in time.

PEG: All I have — all I've ever had is memories — just memories … and memories of memories. *(Pause)* I was raped on my twelfth birthday. *(Pause)* I was twelve years old and as innocent as that caricature of a pig in the Flying Pig BBQ sign. *(Pause)* I remember wearing a pink taffeta dress and twirling, twirling, twirling. I remember girls giggling. And boys. I remember the boys. *(Pause)* I remember clowns and cupcakes and candles. I remember blowing out twelve candles shaped like tiny pink ballerinas, wafting away a lifetime of innocence. And the next day I woke up, remembering nothing but the sense of helplessness … the hopelessness of despair. *(Pause)*

And that's it — other than the nightmares and the fleeting glimpse of two dark shapes racing into the blackness of the night — that's all I remember. That's all I've ever remembered. There are just too many dark gray paths leading nowhere, too many shadows, too many muddy footprints to sort out and all my memories are of shadows, pink shadows, taffeta shadows and other than that, there's nothing. Nothing! *(Pause)*

The following year I was in Gloucester, Massachusetts, and it was my thirteenth birthday. Mother lit a candle and stuck it off-center in a Hostess cream-filled cupcake and the filling oozed out the side and dribbled over the plate. And I watched as the chocolate melted, reeking of tar and it was something so strange, so macabre, that it was unforgettably … forgettable. My yellow cat, whose name I've racked my mind trying to remember, the one with three white boots and a dark brown ear, struggled from my lap, whacked the candle with its paw, licked off the white icing, and devoured the creamy smooth filling and I didn't care. I just didn't care. When I looked around, I realized something was gone and I didn't know what it was back then — but I know now: It was my childhood. My childlike soul had been stolen in the middle of the night. Puff, gone, kaput, snatched away forever. *(Pause)*

I woke up a woman, a lost soul struggling to find the missing puzzle of my life. Now all I remember is that mysterious smell, never quite able to breathe deeply enough to know what it was — not knowing who I was or who I am even though I've spent the past ten years searching for those lost memories, sniffing for that smell, looking for that winding gray path, all I ever find are a thousand narrow lanes funneling into nothingness as each moment fades into an abysmal color of gray-black, black-gray, ebony-black-gray ... into the blackness of the deepest, blackest black hole. And I wake up alone and screaming in the dark gray night, in a place where white and black are smudged together, obliterating, eradicating, erasing everything inside me, erasing my memory, as the paths and the smells morph into a noxious ... an obnoxious smudge pot, filling my soul with pungent gray smoke, inundating me with soot. *(Pause)*

And then it ends. The last flickering bits of memory fade and I'm left wandering in the woods alone ... alone and unprotected. And those are my memories. My memories of memories.

But I survive! I shall always survive!

That's who I am! That's what I'll always be!

Waiting for Grass to Grow
by Bronwyn Barnwell

In this original duo scene, a young boy in his late teens sits quietly outside on a bench with his head resting in his hands. It is dark and only the moon and a single street lamp cast any light on the scene. A young girl also in her late teens silently enters and slowly approaches the bench. They sit on opposite sides of the bench. A flood of mingled emotions slowly unfolds as the two apparent strangers share an intimate, hushed conversation that builds steadily to an unexpected "twist" ending ... further deepening the mystery of this chance encounter.

The young teens offer a compelling portrait of two modern soul mates who move from a casual encounter to a deeper, more profound sense of compassion and "coming of age" that is strengthened and enhanced in the final poignant moment. Throughout there is a bittersweet, deeply human aura of real human beings helplessly at the mercy of events and feelings beyond their control ... but who seem to be reaching out to each other for understanding of what lies ahead.

MARCY: *(Sits awkwardly at first, facing away from the boy, who does not look at her either. She searches for something to say. Finally she turns towards the boy, takes a deep breath, and slowly speaks.)* You know when I was nine a boy down the street from me died. He was twelve and had big blue eyes. I never knew him well, but he was always nice to me.

LANCE: *(Looks confused.)* Why are you telling me this?

MARCY: *(Considers going on with her story but reconsiders.)* When do you get the call?

LANCE: No idea. Just a lot of waiting. *(Angry)* I just want it to be over. I want it all done with.

MARCY: *(Softly)* You don't mean that.

LANCE: *(Looks as if he will yell at her, but then softens.)* You're right. I don't. I never want this call to come. I've been hoping for five years now that this call wouldn't come. Now it seems inevitable.

MARCY: *(There is silence. She looks at him, but he doesn't look back.)* How advanced is the cancer?

LANCE: It was "only a matter of time" two years ago. Ever since she's been treated like a ticking bomb. *(He is quiet for a moment, and then his face hardens with determination.)* I wish I could have it. I wish I could be ill for her. To see that woman suffer, she's the sweetest *(Voice break)* creature on earth.

MARCY: When did you last see her?

LANCE: Three months ago. *(Twiddles his thumbs and looks down, ashamed.)* They say I shouldn't fly back now, that we might miss each other and that would be too hard to bear. I can't help but think about the last thing I said to her.

MARCY: *(Waits a moment to see if he will tell her, but then decides to ask.)* What was that?

LANCE: Good-bye. It seems so simple. *(Stands up, throwing his arms about.)* So stupid! She deserved more than a good-bye!

MARCY: *(Stands up next to him, reaches out a hand to place on his shoulder, and then pulls back quickly.)* You couldn't have known! Good-bye is a normal response. You can't blame yourself for that!

LANCE: But I can! Everyone always teaches you to say I love you to your mom every chance you get. Why didn't I? Why in that moment did I decide that I was above doing that? *(Slumps back* *down on the bench in defeat.)* Now I can't say I love you. I can't talk to her. I can't see her. I'm just waiting for her to die. *(A long pause. MARCY glances at LANCE several times. She moves back to her spot on the bench, but positions herself so that she is now sitting closer to LANCE than before.)*

MARCY: Have you ever known anyone who died before?

LANCE: No.

MARCY: When Jimmy Sanders did, I was in shock. The only dead people I had ever known were people in movies or other people's grandparents. It hit me hard. I never knew why.

LANCE: Do you know now?

MARCY: No, all I know is that he had a very smooth blue driveway. *(She begins to forget that she is talking to LANCE and drifts back to the past.)* I remember it because it was the only one of its kind. After he died, I would go sit in his driveway and feel the cement. *(She rubs her thigh as she thinks about the cement, her eyes closed.)* Somehow feeling that cement made me feel close to him. I would make up stories about things he would have done on that driveway. Playing hopscotch or frying an egg on a hot day. That's how I kept Jimmy alive. I felt like I had to, like if I didn't, my own mortality would come under question.

LANCE: What did your parents think of that?

MARCY: They never knew. But Jimmy's mom found me one day. I was just sitting there, stroking her driveway. She told me I shouldn't sit there anymore because someone could drive in and I could get really hurt.

LANCE: What did you say? *(LANCE slowly inches closer to MARCY.)*

MARCY: I told her that I couldn't move. And I explained to her about Jimmy.

LANCE: How did she take that?

MARCY: She cried, and she hugged me for a long time. We just sat there in the driveway for what seemed like hours. She told me that Jimmy had scraped his knee a few hundred times and that he had fallen off his bike and gotten a broken ankle once. She said I was the first person she had cried to about Jimmy, and I just held her hand. *(She and LANCE are now sitting next to each other.)*

LANCE: Wow.

MARCY: And then she told me a story. *(She looks confused, as if she's just now remembered an important detail.)*

LANCE: *(Looks concerned.)* What? *(MARCY doesn't answer immediately.)* What's wrong?

MARCY: *(Recovers from her glazed-over state.)* No, nothing's wrong. I had just forgotten about this until now.

LANCE: *(Waiting for her to tell him. When she doesn't, he speaks.)* Well, are you going to tell me? *(He laughs.)*

MARCY: I don't know if you want to hear it. *(She laughs as well. They are now seated very close on the bench.)* It awed a nine-year-old, but I don't know how a college student like you will take it.

LANCE: *(Smiles a really big smile for the first time.)* Try me.

MARCY: Well she said, if I remember correctly, that there once was a little boy and he had a beautiful flower planted in his backyard. *(She uses her arms to paint the picture.)* It was a daisy and this I remember because Jimmy's mom said it was the most magnificent daisy in the world and put all the other daisies to shame. Its petals were long and soft and its center was a shimmery gold that smelled so sweet that one sniff would make all the daily troubles fade away. The boy would go to the daisy every day and would tell the flower his problems and his secrets. *(She pauses and looks at LANCE as if to ask for permission to continue the story.)*

LANCE: *(Giving her the confidence to continue)* And?

MARCY: Then one day, the boy went outside to find that his flower was gone. He looked everywhere, but his beautiful daisy was gone forever. So he went to his mother crying and explained that his daisy was gone forever. She then picked the boy up in her arms and pointed up to the sun and said, "There is your daisy. And every morning he will be there to greet you, and every evening he will be there to kiss you goodnight." *(As she is quoting the mother, MARCY takes LANCE's hand in hers.)*

LANCE: *(Looks down at their hands intertwined and looks back up at MARCY.)* Marcy, I ... *(Before he can finish, a high-pitched ringing phone interrupts him. LANCE and MARCY look at each other for a moment. MARCY nods. The phone rings three more times. LANCE reaches into his pocket. They continue holding hands. MARCY's eyes never leave LANCE's face as he answers the* *phone.)* Hello? *(There is a pause as the other person on the line speaks. LANCE's hold on MARCY's hand becomes tighter.)* I see. *(LANCE hangs up the phone. He sits silently for a moment, looking up at the sky and the moon and inhaling the air around him. He then turns to MARCY, still holding her hand, and whispers in a soft, scared voice that could belong to a little boy.)* So what happens when the sun went down? Who did the little boy talk to?

MARCY: *(Looks up at the moon, trying to find the words to console her friend and then turns back to LANCE.)* I'm not sure. I never asked. *(They look at each other, and LANCE looks away. MARCY takes her free arm and wraps it around LANCE's shoulders, pulling him close.)* But Lance, you know you can always talk to me. *(In a moment of defeat, LANCE lets out a gasp of emotion and buries his face on MARCY's shoulder, sobbing uncontrollably while she rubs his back looking up at the moon.)*

Just a Kiss
by Robin Pond

This original "first kiss" duo scene is a clever comedy that features a young couple at the end of an awkward first date. It is a warm and richly amusing tale of what the future consequences may be after that initial first kiss. Harmon, whimsical and playful with just a dose of seriousness, is leaning in to kiss Melodie, coy and colorful but immensely serious-minded, when she abruptly pulls back and the conversation becomes a larger commentary on youthful attitudes toward commitment, selfhood, and the boundaries of friendship and love as the characters play a spirited game of verbal chess.

It's a lighthearted and sometimes bumpy ride on the road to "true love" as the characters slowly reveal their secret thoughts while voicing adolescent aches and pains, as well as grandiose dreams, while skipping carelessly from moments of wild hilarity to moments of deeply moving self-reflection. Ultimately, they are temporarily united in a shared awareness that life, for all its untidiness and disorder, is meant to be lived — for richer or poorer — one kiss at a time.

(A street, in front of a door. MELODIE and HARMON approach, side by side, awkwardly.)

MELODIE: So … here we are.

HARMON: This is it?

MELODIE: Yes. This is it.

HARMON: Looks like a nice place. Nice neighborhood. How long have you lived here?

MELODIE: Eight … going on nine months. For this stage of my life, it's perfect.

HARMON: Nice. *(A pause.)*

MELODIE: So … I had a really good time tonight.

HARMON: Me too.

MELODIE: That was a great little restaurant.

HARMON: Wasn't it?

MELODIE: And so out of the way. How'd you ever find it?

HARMON: Got a flyer in the mail.

MELODIE: Really?

HARMON: Yeah.

MELODIE: I don't think I've ever found a restaurant that way.

HARMON: It was an impressive flyer. Lots of glossy pictures. Action shots — thick cuts of meat, steam rising off the vegetables, all the friendly, smiling waiters — and the descriptions made every special seem really very special.

MELODIE: Sounds impressive.

HARMON: Yeah. It was. *(A pause.)*

MELODIE: Well, then … good night, Harmon.

HARMON: Right. Good night, Melodie … *(HARMON moves forward to kiss MELODIE. She pulls back.)*

MELODIE: Whoa! What're you doing?

HARMON: I … uh … I just thought … I mean … you said you liked the dinner.

MELODIE: It really wasn't all that great.

HARMON: I know. I was disappointed too.

MELODIE: My vegetables were cold.

HARMON: The portions were small.

MELODIE: But I'm not sure I'd have wanted more.

HARMON: And that waiter was downright surly.

MELODIE: I think he was having a bad day.

HARMON: You got to wonder what this world's coming to, when you can't even trust what you see in a flyer.

MELODIE: I know.

HARMON: But at least dinner gave us something to talk about.

MELODIE: And laugh about.

HARMON: *(Trying to take her in his arms)* Then maybe we can get past the disappointing dinner?

MELODIE: *(Pulling back again)* It's not just the dinner.

HARMON: What then? What's ruining the moment? Is there something stuck in my teeth? I should've known. That happens a lot. It's an orthodontal thing. I knew I should've gone and checked in the mirror before we left the restaurant. But I was afraid to leave you.

MELODIE: Afraid I'd bolt?

HARMON: It wouldn't be the first time.

MELODIE: No. It's nothing like that. Really. Nothing personal, and the dinner was … it was okay.

HARMON: What then?

MELODIE: It's just … well … I need to know, before we — you know — I need to know where this is going.

HARMON: It's just a good-night kiss.

MELODIE: A kiss is never just a kiss. It's a promise. A promise of what the future will hold.

HARMON: That's what I'm trying to find out.

MELODIE: But is this the road we really want to travel down?

HARMON: Nothing ventured —

MELODIE: So we date a few months, then maybe we move in together.

HARMON: Sounds good.

MELODIE: We become a couple. All our friends are couples, too.

HARMON: Some of my friends are singles.

MELODIE: You'll have to lose them.

HARMON: Oh.

MELODIE: Then we inevitably marry. Move to the house in the suburbs.

HARMON: We're living in the suburbs?

MELODIE: Yes. Good schools. Good access to shopping and other conveniences.

HARMON: Or maybe a downtown loft.

MELODIE: No. A downtown loft's no place to raise our kids.

HARMON: We've got kids?

MELODIE: Two. Maybe three.

HARMON: Why not more?

MELODIE: I'll make you get a vasectomy.

HARMON: Ouch!

MELODIE: But we'll have several pets.

HARMON: We need pets too?

MELODIE: Kids have to have pets. Some fish, maybe a hamster, or a rabbit, and a cat —

HARMON: Or a dog. I like dogs.

MELODIE: You'll have to walk the dog every night. Maybe twice a night.

HARMON: Twice?

MELODIE: It might have a bladder infection.

HARMON: Sounds like a lot of responsibility.

MELODIE: Constant worry. And a lot of expense. Life doesn't come cheap.

HARMON: I guess: Mortgage. Two cars. Clothing. Food. We probably won't even be able to eat out much anymore.

MELODIE: No. Not with all the special after-school programs for the kids. Summer camp. Doctors. Orthodontists.

HARMON: Just because dental issues run in my family —

MELODIE: A lifetime of cutting coupons out of flyers. We'll both be working so hard to pay for it all, the years'll go sailing by.

HARMON: All this launched by a single kiss.

MELODIE: An intimate commitment —

HARMON: Mapping out the next ten to twenty years of our lives.

MELODIE: And beyond. Before we know it, we're middle-aged. Then we're old. The kids are grown and gone. And we're left there, all alone, in that big rambling house. Just the two of us.

HARMON: Just the two of us.

MELODIE: *(Moving closer. Taking HARMON's hand.)* And I've got to know, when we're left there in the greying light — I've got to know — will there still be as strong a bond between us?

HARMON: *(Takes MELODIE in his arms again.)* There's only one way to find out.

MELODIE: You mean — ?

HARMON: Give me a little kiss, and we'll say good night.

MELODIE: And you'll call me in the morning?

HARMON: Maybe.

MELODIE: Maybe?

HARMON: Yeah ... Maybe. I don't like to plan that far ahead.

(End)

SUPPLEMENTAL RESOURCE MATERIALS

The following resource materials are recommended for actors who may wish additional information on ordering catalogues for the acting edition of a script, monologue anthologies, textbooks on auditions or acting, or securing subscriptions for trade magazines.

Catalogues

Dramatists Play Service, Inc.
440 Park Avenue South
New York, NY 10016
(212) 683-8960
www.dramatists.com

Theatre Communications Group
520 Eighth Avenue
24th Floor
New York, NY 10018
(212) 609-5900
tcg@tcg.org

Samuel French, Inc.
45 West 25th Street
New York, NY 10010
(212) 206-8990
www.samuelfrench.com

Playscripts, Inc.
450 Seventh Avenue
Suite 809
New York, NY 10123
1-866-639-7529
info@playscripts.com

Dramatic Publishing
311 Washington Street
Woodstock, IL 60098
1-800-448-7469
plays@dramaticpublishing.com

Applause Theatre Books
Hal Leonard Corporation
P.O. Box 13819
Milwaukee, WI 53213

Books

Acting One. Robert Cohen. McGraw Hill Publishers, 2007.
Acting in Person and in Style. Jerry L. Crawford, Catherine Hurst, and Michael Lugering. Waveland Press, 2010.
Acting: Thought into Action. Kurt Daw. Heinemann Publishers, 2004.
The Voice Book. Kate Devore and Starr Cookman. Chicago Review Press, 2009.
Free to Act: An Integrated Approach to Acting. Mira Felner. Allyn & Bacon, Inc., 2003.
Voice for the Performer. Linda Gates. Limelight Press, 2009.
Simply Acting: A Handbook for Beginning Actors. Amy Glazer. Kendall Hunt, Inc., 2011.
Audition Success. Don Greene. Theatre Arts Books, 2001.
Tackling Text and Subtext. Barbara Houseman. Theatre Communications Group, 2008.
The Science of Acting. Sam and Helen Kogan. Taylor & Francis, 2009.
Acting: The Basics. Bella Merlin. Routledge Publishers, 2010.
Acting and Reacting: Tools for the Modern Actor. Nick Moseley. Theatre Communications Group, 2006.
The Theatre Audition Book 2. Gerald Lee Ratliff. Meriwether Publishing, 2009.

Subscriptions

American Theatre Magazine
Theatre Communications Group
520 Eighth Avenue
24th Floor
New York, NY 10018

Art Search Magazine
Theatre Communications Group
520 Eighth Avenue
24th Floor
New York, NY 10018

Back Stage
770 Broadway
7th Floor
New York, NY 10003

Dramatics Magazine
2343 Auburn Avenue
Cincinnati, OH 45219

Electronic Resources

Internet Theatre Bookshop
Catalogue of Playscripts
stageplays.com

Theatre Web Resources
Virtual Library
Vl-theatre.com

Artslynx International
Online Theatre Resources
rfinkelso@msn.com

Internet Public Library
Online Texts Collection
www.ipl.org

Actor Tips
Audition Hints
info@actortips.com

LEGAL ACKNOWLEDGMENTS

Copyright Caution

Copyright laws exist to protect the creative and intellectual property rights of creators of original works. All creative works, such as scripts, are considered copyrighted. There are, however, a number of "fair use" exceptions for educational or instructional purposes related to classroom performance. The scripts in this volume are fully protected under the copyright laws of the United States, the British Empire, the Dominion of Canada, and all other countries of the Copyright Union. For additional information related to auditions, full-scale productions, or other available scripts, please contact the author or the author's agent at the address listed.

Chapter 1 Audition Etiquette

I Ate the Divorce Papers by Gabriel Benjamin Davis. Copyright © 2004 by Gabriel Benjamin Davis. Reprinted by permission of the author. For additional information please contact the author at gabriel@alumni.cmu.edu or at gabrielbdavis.com.

Schoolhouse Rock by Jason D. Martin. Copyright © 2001 by Jason D. Martin. Reprinted by permission of the author. For additional information please contact the author at jason.martin@yahoo.com or at www.dramaticwriter.com.

Rhyming and *Driving* by David Moberg. Copyright © 2009 by David Moberg. Reprinted by permission of the author. For additional information please contact the author at dmoberg@irsc.edu or at 164 N.E. Royce Avenue, Port St. Lucie, Florida 34983.

Dating Hamlet by Bruce Kane. Copyright © 2008 by Bruce Kane. Reprinted by permission of the author. For additional information please contact the author at bk@kaneprod.com.

Popcorn, in *Tales from the Tunnel*, by Troy Diana and James Valletti. Copyright © 2008 by Troy Diana and James Valletti. Reprinted by permission of the authors. For additional information please contact Troy Diana at 437 Hyacinth Court, Apt. 303, Altamonte Springs, Florida 32714 or James Valletti at 11 Jeanette Avenue, Staten Island, New York 10312.

No Respect by Bronwyn Barnwell. Copyright © 2011 by Bronwyn Barnwell. Reprinted by permission of the author. For additional information please contact the author at 14 Mustang Mesa, Santa Fe, New Mexico 87506.

Inquest by G.L. Horton. Copyright © 2003 by G.L. Horton. Reprinted by permission of the author. For additional information please contact the author at glhorton@stagepage.info.

Chapter 2 Songs of Fire and Ice

When It Rains Gasoline by Jason D. Martin. Copyright © 2000 by Jason D. Martin. Reprinted by permission of the author. For additional information please contact the author at jason.martin@yahoo.com or at www.dramaticwriter.com.

Lost and Found by Dori Appel. Copyright © 2001 by Dori Appel. Reprinted by permission of the author. For additional information please contact the author at P.O. Box 1364, Ashland, Oregon 97520 or at dori.appel@gmail.com.

The Subway by John Augustine. Copyright © 2007 by John Augustine. Reprinted by permission of the author and International Creative Management. For additional information please contact the author's agent at International Creative Management, 825 Eighth Avenue, New York, New York 10019.

The Stronger Bond by Kristine McGovern. Copyright © 2007 by Kristine McGovern. Reprinted by permission of the author. For additional information please contact the author at krisannmcgovern@gmail.com.

Safe by Deborah Finkelstein. Copyright © 2008 by Deborah Finkelstein. Reprinted by permission of the author. For additional information please contact the author at play@deborahfinkelstein.com.

Chapter 3 Songs of Regret and Romance

Equivocation by Bill Cain. Copyright © 2008 by Bill Cain. Reprinted by permission of the author and Abrams Artists Agency. For additional information please contact the author's agent at Abrams Artists Agency, 275 Seventh Avenue, 26th Floor, New York, New York 10001.

Gee's Bend by Elyzabeth Gregory Wilder. Copyright © 2007 by Elyzabeth Gregory Wilder. Reprinted by permission of the author and Abrams Artists Agency. For additional information please contact the author's agent at Abrams Artists Agency, 275 Seventh Avenue, 26th Floor, New York, New York 10001.

Broken by Barbara Lhota. Copyright © 2005 by Barbara Lhota. Reprinted by permission of the author. For additional information please contact the author at barblhota@gmail.com.

Empty by Julie Halston and Donna Daley. Copyright © 2011 by Julie Halston and Donna Daley. Reprinted by permission of the authors. For additional information please contact Julie Halston at JulieLHalston@gmail.com or Donna Daley at Donyard628@aol.com.

Waiting for Oprah by Mary Miller. Copyright © 2005 by Mary Miller. Reprinted by permission of the author. For additional information please contact the author at mary@marymillerwriter.com or at www.marymillerwriter.com.

Blue Window by Craig Lucas. Copyright © 2003 by Craig Lucas. Reprinted by permission of the Theatre Communications Group. For additional information please contact the publisher at Theatre Communications Group, 520 Eighth Avenue, 24th Floor, New York, New York 10018.

Tomorrow's Wish by Wade Bradford. Copyright © 2011 by Wade Bradford. Reprinted by permission of the author. For additional information please contact the author at wadebradford.com or at profwade@hotmail.com.

Baby's Blues by Tammy Ryan. Copyright © 2006 by Tammy Ryan. Reprinted by permission of the author. For additional information please contact the author's agent at the Susan Gurman Literary Agency, 245 West 99th Street, Suite 24 A, New York, New York 10025.

The Adventure, from *Briefs: 7 Short Plays,* by Eric Lane. Copyright © 2011 by Eric Lane. Reprinted by permission of the author. For additional information please contact the author's agent at The Gersh Agency, 41 Madison Avenue, 33rd Floor, New York, New York 10010.

Miss Witherspoon by Christopher Durang. Copyright © 2005 by Christopher Durang. Reprinted by permission of Grove/Atlantic, Inc. For additional information please contact the publisher at Grove/Atlantic, Inc., 841 Broadway, 4th Floor, New York, New York 10003.

The Baptist Gourmet by Jill Morley. Copyright © 1998 by Jill Morley. Reprinted by permission of the author. For additional information please contact the author at sambano@gmail.com.

The Soy Answer by Carolyn West. Copyright © 1998 by Carolyn West. Reprinted by permission of the author and Brooklyn Publishers. The script may be obtained in its complete ten-minute form from Brooklyn Publishers, P.O. Box 248, Cedar Rapids, Iowa 52406 or you may visit their website at www.brookpub.com.

My Parents by Joe McCabe. Copyright © 2004 by Joe McCabe. Reprinted by permission of the author. For additional information please contact the author at 82 Manassas Drive, Falling Waters, West Virginia 25419.

Doubt by John Patrick Shanley. Copyright © 2008 by John Patrick Shanley. Reprinted by permission of the Theatre Communications Group. For additional information please contact the publisher at Theatre Communications Group, 520 Eighth Avenue, 24th Floor, New York, New York 10018.

Freedom High by Adam Kraar. Copyright © 2006 by Adam Kraar. Reprinted by permission of the author. For additional information please contact the author's agent at the Elaine Devlin Literacy Agency, 20 West 23rd Street, Suite 3, New York, New York 10010.

Mr. Lucky's by Stephen Fife. Copyright © 2005 by Stephen Fife. Reprinted by permission of the author. For additional information please contact the author at slfife@aol.com or at P.O. Box 5425, Santa Monica, California 90409.

Chapter 4 Songs of Illusion and Reality

The Weir by Conor McPherson. Copyright © 2004 by Conor McPherson. Reprinted by permission of Nick Hern Books. For additional information please contact the publisher at Nick Hern Books, The Glasshouse, 49A Goldhawk Road, London W12, 8QP, England.

Glass Eels by Nell Leyshon. Copyright © 2007 by Nell Leyshon. Reprinted by permission of Oberon Books. For additional information please contact the publisher at Oberon Books, 521 Caledonian Road, London N7, 9RH, England.

Tales from the Arabian Mice by Will Averill. Copyright © 2007 by Will Averill. Reprinted by permission of the author and Playscripts, Inc. For additional information, including the purchase of acting editions of the script or to obtain stock and amateur performance rights, please contact Playscripts, Inc. at http://www.playscripts.com or phone 1-866-NEW PLAY (639-7529).

Phantom Rep by Ben Alexander. Copyright © 1994, 2011 by Ben Alexander. Reprinted by permission of the author. For additional information please contact the author at benalexandernyc@yahoo.com.

The Baltimore Waltz by Paula Vogel. Copyright © 1995 by Paula Vogel. Reprinted by permission of the Theatre Communications Group. For additional information please contact the publisher at Theatre Communications Group, 520 Eighth Avenue, 24th Floor, New York, New York 10018.

Sheets of Rain by Lexanne Leonard. Copyright © 2009 by Lexanne Leonard. Reprinted by permission of the author. For additional information please contact the author at 20445 E. Crestline Place, Centennial, Colorado 80015.

Men & Cars by Diane Spodarek. Copyright © 2003 by Diane Spodarek. Reprinted by permission of the author. For additional information please contact the author at diane.spodarek@gmail.com.

Senior Square by John-Michael Williams. Copyright © 1987 by Applause Theatre and Cinema Books, LLC. Reprinted by permission of Hal Leonard Corporation. For additional information please contact the publisher at Hal Leonard Corporation, 7777 West Bluemound Road, P.O. Box 13819, Milwaukee, Wisconsin 53213.

A Day of Turning by Todd Caster. Copyright © 2007 by Todd Caster. Reprinted by permission of the author. For additional information please contact the author at wordcaster@aol.com.

Cruising Close to Crazy by Laura Shaine Cunningham. Copyright © 2002 by Laura Shaine Cunningham. Reprinted by permission of the author. For additional information please contact the author at laurashaine@gmail.com.

The School Mascot by Amanda Kozik. Copyright © 1999 by Amanda Kozik. Reprinted by permission of the author. For additional information please contact the author at amanda_kozik@yahoo.com.

We Cannot Know the Mind of God by Mikhail Horowitz. Copyright © 2002 by Mikhail Horowitz. Reprinted by permission of the author. For additional information please contact the author at horowitz@bard.edu or at 302 High Falls Road, Saugerties, New York 12477.

The Gazing Ball by Dwight Watson. Copyright © 2011 by Dwight Watson. Reprinted by permission of the author. For additional information please contact the author at Wabash College, Crawfordsville, Indiana 47933.

Chapter 5 Songs of Faith and Folly

Reckless by Craig Lucas. Copyright © 2008 by Craig Lucas. Reprinted by permission of the Theatre Communications Group. For additional information please contact Theatre Communications Group, 520 Eighth Avenue, 24th Floor, New York, New York 10018.

Chapter 6 Songs of Rage and Retribution

Stamping, Shouting, and Singing Home by Lisa Evans. Copyright © 2006 by Lisa Evans. Reprinted by permission of Oberon Books. For additional information please contact the publisher at Oberon Books, 521 Caledonian Road, London N7 9RH, England.

Through a Cloud by Jack Shepherd. Copyright © 2005 by Jack Shepherd. Reprinted by permission of Nick Hern Books. For additional information please contact Nick Hern Books, The Glasshouse, A9a Goldhawk Road, London W 12 8QP, England.

Foreign Bodies by Susan Yankowitz. Copyright © 2011 by Susan Yankowitz. Reprinted by permission of the author. For additional information please contact the author at syankowitz@aol.com.

Phat Girls by Debbie Lamedman. Copyright © 2005 by Debbie Lamedman. Reprinted by permission of the author. For additional information please contact the author at debbielamedman@gmail.com or at www.debbielamedman.com.

Sister Santa by Jim Chevallier. Copyright © 1997 by Jim Chevallier. Reprinted by permission of the author. For additional information, including the author's collections of monologues for teens and twenties, please contact the author at jimchev@chezjim.com.

Cutting Remarks by Barbara Lhota. Copyright © 2004 by Barbara Lhota. Reprinted by permission of the author. For additional information please contact the author at barblhota@gmail.com.

Whalesong in My Latte by Jennifer DiMarco. Copyright © 1997 by Jennifer DiMarco. Reprinted by permission of the author. For additional information please contact the author at jennifer@orchardhousepress.com.

August: Osage County by Tracy Letts. Copyright © 2008 by Tracy Letts. Reprinted by permission of the Theatre Communications Group. For additional information please contact Theatre Communications Group, 520 Eighth Avenue, 24th Floor, New York, New York 10018.

Of Course They Call It a Tragedy by Gus Edwards. Copyright © 1997 by Gus Edwards. Reprinted by permission of the author. For additional information please contact the author's agent at the Susan Schulman Literary Agency, 454 West 44th Street, New York, New York 10036.

The Eros Trilogy by Nicky Silver. Copyright © 2000 by Nicky Silver. Reprinted by permission of the Theatre Communications Group. For additional information please contact Theatre Communications Group, 520 Eighth Avenue, 24th Floor, New York, New York 10018.

Bludgeon the Lime by Michael Weems. Copyright © 2011 by Michael Weems. Reprinted by permission of the author and JAC Publishing & Promotions, P.O. Box 88, Burlington, Massachusetts 01803. For additional information please contact the author at michaeltw721@gmail.com.

Unbroken Heart by Scot Walker. Copyright © 2011 by Scot Walker. Reprinted by permission of the author. For additional information please contact the author at scotwalker2004@yahoo.com.

About the Editor

Gerald Lee Ratliff is the award-winning author of numerous journal articles, essays, and textbooks in classroom teaching strategies and performance studies. He has served as President of the Speech and Theatre Association of New Jersey; Eastern Communication Association; Association of Communication Administration; and Theta Alpha Phi, a national theatre fraternity. He has also served on administrative and editorial boards of the American Council of Academic Deans, International Arts Association, National Communication Association, Eastern Communication Association, and the Society of Educators and Scholars.

He was awarded the "Distinguished Service Award" by both the Eastern Communication Association and Theta Alpha Phi; named a Fulbright Scholar to China; selected as a U.S.A. delegate of the John F. Kennedy Center for the Performing Arts to Russia; and has received multiple teaching awards for pioneering innovative curriculum design, pedagogy, and instructional practices. He is currently active as a program consultant in higher education administration and a frequent keynote speaker and workshop facilitator at national academic and professional conferences.

Order Form

Meriwether Publishing Ltd.
PO Box 7710
Colorado Springs, CO 80933-7710
Phone: 800-937-5297 Fax: 719-594-9916
Website: www.meriwether.com

Please send me the following books:

_____ **Audition Monologues for Young Women** **$16.95**
#BK-B323
edited by Gerald Lee Ratliff
Contemporary audition pieces for aspiring actresses

_____ **Young Women's Monologs from** **$15.95**
Contemporary Plays #BK-B272
edited by Gerald Lee Ratliff
Professional auditions for aspiring actresses

_____ **Young Women's Monologues from** **$15.95**
Contemporary Plays #2 #BK-B300
edited by Gerald Lee Ratliff
Professional auditions for aspiring actresses

_____ **Acting Scenes and Monologs for** **$15.95**
Young Women #BK-B228
by Maya Levy
A collection of monologs and scenes for young women

_____ **50/50 Monologues for Student Actors** **$15.95**
#BK-B321
by Mary Depner
100 monologues for guys and girls

_____ **102 Great Monologues #BK-B315** **$16.95**
by Rebecca Young
A versatile collection of monologues and duologues for student actors

These and other fine Meriwether Publishing books are available at
your local bookstore or direct from the publisher. Prices subject to
change without notice. Check our website or call for current prices.

Name: _____ email:_____

Organization name: _____

Address: _____

City: _____ State: _____

Zip: _____ Phone: _____

❏ **Check enclosed**

❏ **Visa / MasterCard / Discover / Am. Express #** _____

Signature: _____ *Expiration date:* _____ / _____
(required for credit card orders)

Colorado residents: Please add 3% sales tax.
Shipping: Include $3.95 for the first book and 75¢ for each additional book ordered.

❏ *Please send me a copy of your complete catalog of books and plays.*

Order Form

Meriwether Publishing Ltd.
PO Box 7710
Colorado Springs, CO 80933-7710
Phone: 800-937-5297 Fax: 719-594-9916
Website: www.meriwether.com

Please send me the following books:

_____ **Audition Monologues for Young Women** **$16.95**
#BK-B323
edited by Gerald Lee Ratliff
Contemporary audition pieces for aspiring actresses

_____ **Young Women's Monologs from** **$15.95**
Contemporary Plays #BK-B272
edited by Gerald Lee Ratliff
Professional auditions for aspiring actresses

_____ **Young Women's Monologues from** **$15.95**
Contemporary Plays #2 #BK-B300
edited by Gerald Lee Ratliff
Professional auditions for aspiring actresses

_____ **Acting Scenes and Monologs for** **$15.95**
Young Women #BK-B228
by Maya Levy
A collection of monologs and scenes for young women

_____ **50/50 Monologues for Student Actors** **$15.95**
#BK-B321
by Mary Depner
100 monologues for guys and girls

_____ **102 Great Monologues #BK-B315** **$16.95**
by Rebecca Young
A versatile collection of monologues and duologues for student actors

**These and other fine Meriwether Publishing books are available at
your local bookstore or direct from the publisher. Prices subject to
change without notice. Check our website or call for current prices.**

Name: _____ email:_____

Organization name: _____

Address: _____

City: _____ State: _____

Zip: _____ Phone: _____

❑ **Check enclosed**

❑ **Visa / MasterCard / Discover / Am. Express #** _____

Signature: _____ *Expiration
date:* _____ / _____
(required for credit card orders)

Colorado residents: Please add 3% sales tax.
Shipping: Include $3.95 for the first book and 75¢ for each additional book ordered.

❑ *Please send me a copy of your complete catalog of books and plays.*